THINGS I HAVE LEARNED

Chapel Talks at
Bob Jones University

by

BOB JONES, D.D., LL.D.

DEDICATED

TO

"my Boys and Girls"

wherever they are

PREFACE . . .

THE TWENTY MESSAGES in this volume are a few of the many Chapel talks which I have given to our own Bob Jones College students. We have made no effort to edit these messages. They were mechanically recorded (some of them without my knowing at the time that they were being recorded) and are being released in the exact form in which they were given. The friends who read the addresses will notice that we often mention Bob Jones College, but they will, of course, understand that we were talking to our own students and were endeavoring to drill into them not only the principles under discussion but also the spirit of the institution of which the author is the founder.

Having had a wide experience over a period of many years in dealing with thousands of people in the various walks of life, I am fully convinced that even the *average* Christian can be "a success" in the field of service to which he is Divinely called if he will "live up to" the practical philosophy which is emphasized in these addresses.

BOB JONES.

TABLE OF CONTENTS

～∽～

Things I Have Learned

No. 1

I WANT this morning to drill into you some of the little philosophy of life for which I stand and for which this college stands—the philosophy I have gathered up along life's way.

I do not claim to be a scholar. I haven't had time to be a scholar. I have moved too fast. I have been too busy. I haven't had the time with books I wish I could have had. I love good books. I love literature. I love music. I love art. But God has called me to a strenuous, busy life; and I haven't had time to be the scholar I should like to be. I have read all I could, even on trains as I have traveled over the country. I have tried not to waste my time. When I have had an opportunity I have looked into good books, but I have had to do it in a hurry.

While I haven't lived with books, I have lived with people. Though I am not a scholar, I do know people. I know what people think. I know the mental processes of the masses of people. I am going to tell you this morning and in some other messages to follow some of the things I have learned in dealing with people.

Every successful person I have ever met had come at some time in his life under the dominating power of some great truth. If you succeed in this world it is going to be because sometime you hear something, or you see something, or you get an idea that grips your very soul. If you meet a great man anywhere in this world and ask that great man, "How did you succeed?" he will answer "One time I heard somebody say something and I began to think about it"; or he will say, "One time I came across something in a book"; or "One time I was walking along and got an idea and that idea made me." You will find that is always true. If you go to Mr. Henry Ford at the head of probably the greatest private business in the world and say, "Mr. Ford, you are an old man. I want to ask you a question: How did you get to be a successful business-man?" Mr. Ford will say, "Well, one day a certain idea came to me."

Years ago there lived in this country a unique platform man. He was a great preacher. No man could excel him in the pulpit when he really preached. That man was named Sam Jones. He was brought up down in Georgia, just a few miles from Cleveland, Tennessee. Sam Jones was a little country Methodist circuit-rider. One day he went to hear a man by the name of Simon Peter Richardson. Simon Peter Richardson was a very unique personality, well known throughout this southern country. Sam Jones, just a little country circuit-rider, sat there and listened to that unique man preach. Sam's face lighted up. Then he looked as if he were thinking. His face lighted up again. When the sermon was over Sam walked out and said to a crowd of young preachers, "Boys, I have learned something today. I have learned that the pulpit is not a prison but a throne. I have learned that the preacher is not a prisoner; the preacher is a king with a scepter. He is on a throne of power!" Sam Jones became probably the greatest platform man America ever produced.

If you succeed in life you are going to see something, you are going to hear something, or you are going to get an idea that will make you. What is the greatest idea you ever had? What is the greatest lesson you ever learned?

I am going to tell you the greatest thought I ever had. It is a simple little thing. One time as a country boy I was walking down a road. Suddenly it occurred to me that *I had to live somewhere forever*. Of course, I had known that. The Bible taught me that. My mother had told me that. The Sunday School teacher had told me that. But I had never realized it before. It dawned on me in a moment that I had to live somewhere forever. I said to myself, "It doesn't matter whether I want to live or not. I may prefer to die and sleep a dreamless sleep in the silent dust, but I can't do it. I've got to live. I've got to live as long as God Almighty lives. I've got to live until God dies. I've got to live until angels sing a funeral dirge over His grave. Like it or not like it, I've got to live." I said, "Since I've got to live, I had better learn how to live."

A young man came to me one time and said, "Life isn't worth living. I am in trouble. I am a failure." I said, "How old are you?" He said, "Thirty years old." Think of a man thirty years old saying life isn't worth living! I am sixty, and let me tell you something. Life was never as interesting as it is to me now. I have a thousand jobs I want to do and a thousand dreams I am dreaming. Talk about life not being worth living! Think of a fellow's ending his own life—committing suicide!

That fellow said, "I am going to end my life." I said, "How are you going to end your life?" He said, "I am going to blow my brains out." I said, "You can't blow your brains out; you haven't any brains to blow out." He looked at me and said, "Don't make fun of me. Don't laugh at me. I am going to end my life." I said, "You can't end it. You can blow a hole in your head. You can get up on the house and jump off. You can close the doors, stop all the cracks, and turn on the gas. You can go uptown and buy some strychnine at the drug store and take it. But *you can't stop living*. We will take your old body and put you to bed with a shovel and throw dirt in your face, but you can't stop living!"

Young people, listen to me! You've got to live. Like it or not like it, *you have got it to do!* You have to live forever and forever and forever!

You are a fool if you don't learn how to live. That is what is the matter with the world: people do not know how to live. We have been building schools and colleges and all sorts of technical institutions to teach people how to make a living. But a few years ago the highways of America were crowded with university graduates who couldn't make a living. Anybody can make a living now under war conditions. Uncle Sam makes a living for you now. But there are hard days ahead of you. Jobs will be scarce. Mark my word, you will see the time when it will take character to hold a job. You don't have to have character to hold one now, but you will see another day in this country when efficiency will be in demand and character will be what folks are looking for.

A few years ago university presidents would make commencement addresses and say, "Young ladies and young gentlemen, you are up against it. I am sorry for you." At that time I stood on the platform and offered anybody a thousand dollars who would find one graduate of Bob Jones College out of work, unless he were sick. When these highways were crowded with university graduates who couldn't get a job, a graduate of Bob Jones College without a good position could not be found. The reason was that Bob Jones College teaches people how to live. That is the greatest lesson in the world. We teach science. We teach literature. We teach history. We teach all the academic subjects. But we teach students how to live.

Some of the biggest "nuts" I ever met in my life were Doctors of Philosophy. I had a letter one time from a man who said, "I have a Doctor of Philosophy degree from a certain great university and my wife has a Doctor of Philosophy degree from another university. My major was in a certain field and her major was in another field. Both of us are out of work. I had a position in a school and couldn't hold it. My wife had a position and couldn't hold it. We are misfits. We have tried and tried and tried to get a job. We are hungry. We have nothing to eat. If you will give us a place to sleep and something to eat, we will come and teach in Bob Jones College." That is pitiful. It is bad enough to have a "Ph.D." married to a "Ph.D.," but think of two "Ph.D.'s" without any common sense and unable to make a living!

There is something wrong with the present system of education. When the scholars and educational leaders were making the greatest effort ever made on earth to teach people how to make a living there were more college and university graduates out of work than at any other time in the history of the country. Put this back in a pigeonhole of your brain and let it stay there: I have had a wide experience *and I have never yet found a man who knew how to live who ever had any trouble making a living. If you will learn how to live, you can make a living.*

I believe in home economics. But my old country mother could make better biscuits than any home economics teachers on the American continent. She could fry the best ham and scramble the best eggs. She could make the best sweet potato custard and the most wonderful cake—she could sugar-coat every bit of it exactly right! And she never saw a home economics teacher!

My old country father never attended an agricultural school in his life, but he knew how to tickle the ground and make it smile with harvest. He could produce yam potatoes as big as you ever saw, and ears of corn that made the neighbors almost worship at the granary shrine.

You learn how to live! Learning to cook is easy. Learning to plow is easy. You think it is hard to learn mathematics. That is easy. You think Greek and Hebrew are hard. They are easy. You learn to live! You can graduate from college and go through the graduate school and be a fool. And we are not turning out fools! We let the fools go before they finish! This is not a "nut" factory!

A good old saint, a well-educated man, died years ago. He had read everything. He knew all the books. He could tell a person anything he wanted to know. He died. His remains were brought into the church. The preacher got up and said, "My dear Brethren, Mr. So-and-So is not here in the coffin. He is with the Lord. This is just the shell, the old 'nut' is in Heaven."

We don't tolerate in Bob Jones College slovenly work in the classroom. You can't skim over the job here and get away with it. We want you to study hard and do a good job not for just what you are going to learn in books. We want you to build your character by that effort. If you haven't taken some subject in college that you hate, I am tempted to hate you. Any student who comes to a college like this and doesn't take something he despises has no business being in college. If you like music, take music. If you hate mathematics, take mathematics. Offset one with the other. Build character. Learn how to live!

A lot of people are going to heaven when they die— and the sooner the better! They are going to make it. God is awfully good. His grace is so wonderful. But there are a lot of saved people who do not know how to live. They can't fit into any situation. They can't get along anywhere. A man said to me one day, "I just can't get along with that old maid. I just can't work in the organization with her." I said, "Well, what is the matter with you?" He said, "What is the matter with me? Nothing. What is the matter with her?"

When I can't get along with people personally I always figure there is something wrong with me. Of course there are times when my convictions about what is right create friction. But that is not personal. That is principle. I have learned never to "pass the buck" to somebody else. If I can't fit in I don't blame the hole. I blame myself. People say you can't fit a round peg into a square hole or a square peg into a round hole. Well, if God has a round hole for you and you are a square peg, you ought to turn into a round peg. If God has a square hole which He wants you to fit into and you are a round peg, square up and get in!

Now, hurriedly I will give you a few of the practical things I have learned along life's way.

No man ever succeeds in life who does not learn to finish every job he undertakes. Finish the job! Finish the job!! Don't shine one shoe and leave the other one unshined. Shine both of them! Don't wash one ear and leave the other one dirty. Don't pull out the eyebrows over one eye, you girls, and not pull them out over the other eye. If you are going to act the fool, go the "whole hog." Don't have any fights you can get out of having. But if you have to fight, go through with it. Do a good job!

I used to have a friend who was always in a fight and, strange to say, he licked every man he fought. One day I asked him how he did it. He said, "It is easy—get in a good lick and get done with it." Joe Louis might give you some lessons on finishing the job. He didn't mess around when he had it to do. He did it.

Here is a college girl who goes to her room at night. She says, "I have a hard day tomorrow. I must get my 'math' because that 'math' is hard . . . no, I believe I will get my English. English is awfully hard. The lessons are long, too . . . no, I believe I will get my history . . . well, no, I am going to write John a note!" That is the way she lives—never finishes anything. If that girl does not learn to get down to business and finish something, I pity the poor fool who marries her. Learn while you are young the lessons of finishing the job. If you have something to do, do it and be done with it.

I think I am doing about as much as any one private citizen you ever saw. I write letters every day that take as much mental effort as it takes for the average preacher to prepare both sermons on Sunday. I give a chapel talk every day when I am at home, and once in a while ' say something original. We turn out from our office on an average of a hundred personal letters a day. We are doing a thousand and one things that I couldn't even mention. Somebody said, "How can you do it?" The answer is: Finish every job and get through with it. It is marvelous what a man can do if he will learn while he is young to finish the job. Get through with it. Dismiss it from your mind. Go on about your business. Get done with what you have to do and be done with it.

No doubt the trouble is with you! Young people, don't start out in life blaming anybody but yourself. Learn to take responsibility. When you fail don't blame the teacher. Don't blame conditions. Don't blame circumstances. Don't make alibis. Start out in life always to take responsibility. You are a Christian, aren't you? You have God to help you, haven't you? You have Omnipotence back of you, don't you? You are trusting God, aren't you? Well, isn't God Almighty greater than any difficulty in life?

A fellow came to my office one time and asked me for financial backing. His shoes were cracked across the top (that was before shoes were rationed). The heels were run-down. His fingernails were dirty. He had a history of sorrow—the whole universe had been organized against him. And he was against everything. He reminded me of the fellow who dropped into a church conference one Saturday. He came in late and sat down. Then he got up and said, "Brother Moderator, I don't know what you are discussing, but put me down as being 'a-gin' it." You have seen these people who are "a-gin" everything. I used to have a friend who gave a lecture on "A-ginits."

This fellow, to hear him tell it, had been mistreated all his life. His mother was mean to him. His old daddy who was dead and gone had treated him bad. His grandmother was a reprobate. His maternal and paternal ancestors had cursed him before he was born! The Republican Party had ruined him and the Democrats had cursed him and spit on him. Prohibition had ruined the country and him, too. I sat there and thought how pitiful it was that the poor, miserable failure would blame everybody in the world, when there was nobody to blame but himself.

There is nobody but you to blame for your failure. Let that sink in. One time a girl in Bob Jones College came in to see me. She said, "One of the teachers has it in for me." "Why," I said, "you are not that important. You have to be somebody before people get it in for you." Of course the devil has it in for you, but God is on your side and God Almighty can make even the wrath of men to praise Him. He can hitch human hatred to your chariot and pull you through all the mud of difficulty. Quit blaming anybody but yourself. You will be a failure if you "pass the buck" to somebody else.

Years ago while conducting an evangelistic campaign in Grand Rapids, Michigan, a man told me about an old "bum" who went to sleep on some whisky barrels in the rear of a saloon. The poor old bum had a beard of almost two weeks' growth. While he slept a man rubbed Limburger cheese into his beard. After awhile he waked up and began to sniffle a little. He smelled his hands. He walked out in the street and whiffed the air. He went on out to the park and plucked a flower and smelled of that. He slowly turned around and started back to town. When he got to town he went into a drug store, went up to the druggist and said, "Would you mind my smelling some of this perfume?" "No," the druggist said, "that is all right. Go right ahead." He opened the bottle, smelled of the perfume, and closed the bottle. He started back down the street and passed a man and said, "He smells bad." He passed a beautiful woman in a fur coat. She had cologne all over her and smelled lovely to everybody else, but to him she smelled awfully bad. He entered a saloon, walked up to the bar and said, "I have one dime, Mister; give me something to drink right quick." The fellow poured out a glass of cheap liquor and handed it to him. He took it and started to drink it and said, "Ain't it awful?" The saloonkeeper said, "Ain't what awful?" The fellow said, "Can't you smell it—the whole world smells rotten!"

Young people, if you smell anything around here it is your own smell. Don't you walk around here and say, "I went to the Dean's office and, say, it just smelled awful! I don't see why people talk about Bob Jones College being such a wonderful place, it surely smells bad to me. I went in to see Dr. Bob Jones and he smelled bad. I went in to see Dr. Bob Jones, Jr., and he smelled worse than his daddy! I just can't get anywhere near that registrar. He is awful. He smells terrible!"

Any smelling you smell around here is your own smell. Don't forget that. Don't you go around "smelling" up this place and then blame somebody else! Wait a minute. I'm not joking. I'm not playing with you. I'm driving something home to you. While you are young don't "pass the buck" for how you smell and what you are. You will be a failure as long as you live if you look at life like that.

We will have another class in practical philosophy here at chapel tomorrow morning. If your professor of philosophy tells you something different, just remember I am talking to you out of life. I did not get this out of books. I think you will probably find that his philosophy and mine are in agreement. I got mine in contact with people through a period of many years, and that is where all the other philosophers got theirs, if they got it right. Let us pray.

Prayer: "Our Heavenly Father, we pray Thee to bless these young people. Help us to walk out of this place this morning with the regenerating influence and power of the Holy Spirit in our lives. Help us to be what we ought to be, true to God and faithful to every responsibility. Lead us in the way Thou wouldst have us go. Keep this college true. Help us to learn all we can from books and do our work well, but help us to remember that if we do not learn to live we shall make a failure in life regardless of whatever else we learn. Help us to succeed, not because we want selfishly to succeed, but because we want to succeed for the glory of God. We ask it in Jesus' name. Amen!"

Things I Have Learned

No. 2

I WANT to talk to you again this morning about some helpful, practical things I have learned along life's way.

Back of every tragedy in human character there is a slow process of wicked thinking. Nobody ever went to ruin and hell suddenly. Every man who ever fell was prepared for the fall by a process of thinking that wasn't right. If you ever go to ruin it will be because you began to think wrong and kept thinking wrong until the fall came. No man ever fell suddenly. No girl ever fell suddenly. The girl who falls like a star out of the sky, falls because she was prepared for the fall. No man ever walked down to a bank, broke the bank open, and robbed it on the spur of the moment without having been prepared mentally ahead of time for the crime. *You had better watch your thoughts!* The folks who think right live right, and the folks who don't live right are folks who don't think right.

The people who succeed are the people who make stepping stones out of stumbling stones. The road of success is a stony road. There never has been a smooth road to success. Piled up on that road are stones to

21

block your way. When you come to a stone, don't stumble over it—step on it, climb up on it! You can do it.

A student is coming down the road and the stone of poverty is in his way. What is he going to do? I heard a boy say last night, "Thank God for hearing my prayers and sending money so I could stay in college." Many of you don't have a financial problem. Most people in this day and time have money. But we have a few students here on faith. This stone of poverty is in their way. What are they going to do? Are they going to say, "We are hard up; we are going home"? Not if they have anything to them. If they have anything to them they will step on that stone of financial hardship.

Somebody else comes along on the road of life—somebody who has fallen desperately in love. His emotions are all upset and he feels that he wants to quit. What will he do? If he has any character he will just step on that rock of emotion and climb on up to a successful life. Learn to make stepping stones out of stumbling stones.

Duties never conflict. I talked to a young man this morning who last summer wrote his sweetheart a long letter every day. Sometimes he wrote her two or three times a day. He wrote his mother a post card. He ought to be ashamed of himself. He ought to have written his sweetheart; but he ought to have written his mother, too. If his sweetheart objected to his dividing his time with his mother, she was not worthy to be any boy's sweetheart. A boy has a duty toward his sweetheart and a duty toward his mother. Duties never conflict.

I read in a paper a day or two ago something interesting. When President Roosevelt was overseas recently, his son, on the order of the Commander-in-Chief of the Army, left his boat and came to his father. He walked into the presence of his father. As a soldier of his country he owed a salute to his Commander-in-Chief. As the son of a father, he owed him a kiss. He paid both debts.

Duties never conflict. I owe a duty to my wife, a duty to my son, a duty to my grandchildren, a duty to my daughter-in-law, a duty to Bob Jones College, a duty to my country, a duty to my God; and in God's universe His commands never conflict—never, under any circumstances. Keep your relations right. When you overpay one obligation by subtracting from another obligation, you are sinning against God.

Every person is either master or mastered. He is either a victor or a victim. He is either a conqueror or he is conquered. What are you? If you don't master your mathematics this semester, your mathematics will master you. If you don't conquer Greek, Greek will conquer you. If you are not a victor in the Hebrew class, you will be a victim in the Hebrew class. And the smaller the thing that masters a man, the greater the reflection on the man. Do you want to know how big you are? If so, find out what holds you down on your back, the thing to which you have surrendered.

I saw a fellow on a train one time. He was sitting across the aisle from me—a little, thin-chested, emaciated, pale-faced fellow. By his side sat a big athlete. This little emaciated fellow would run up to the smoker every few minutes and then come back and sit down.

After awhile he said to the big, husky fellow, "What do you do?" The athlete said, "I play football." The little fellow said, as he stopped to cough, "I wish I could play, but I can't quit cigarettes." I looked at him. There he was—a little, thin-chested, emaciated fellow, flat on his back. Upon his chest was a little cigarette. The cigarette had its little nicotine knee on his chest and its little nicotine fingers on his throat. The fellow said, "I surrender. I surrender!" If a thing ever gets me down I want it to be something big. I would hate to be run over by a little piece of paper or a little tobacco that is guaranteed not to have a scratch for your throat—not a cough in it!

You can borrow brains but you can't borrow character. Successful people are people who know where to borrow brains. Young people, if I have had in this world any degree of success I owe it to the fact that I had enough common sense to know what I couldn't do. Blessed is the man who knows what he can't do. As far as success is concerned, it is just as important that you learn what you can't do as it is that you learn what you can do. There never lived a man who could do everything. I knew a man who one time went into a factory. He didn't have a mechanical mind. He tried and tried and then gave up the idea that he could ever be a mechanic. But he became a salesman. He let the other men make the machinery and he sold the machines. He borrowed the brains of the mechanics to make the machines and they borrowed his brains to sell them.

This college exists today because the founder of the institution had faith in God and knew his own limitations. I went out to borrow the brains of men who knew what to do. I went to the right source. When we started this college we needed a dean with a mathematical mind in order to be educationally accurate. We could not afford to take chances on educational standards. Men come to this institution and marvel at the progress the school has made and the efficiency of the institution. Do you know why it is? It is because we have the right fellow in the right place. If we get a fellow in the wrong place, we put him out and put somebody else in his place. We may use him somewhere else.

If I wanted to go "possum" hunting I wouldn't go down on Broadway in New York and find a fellow who wears a long-tail coat and says "o-possum" to go with me. I would go out here in East Tennessee, find some old farmer with a cur dog, and get him to go with me. A man who says "o-possum" never caught a possum. A fellow who lives in the country, who has a cur dog, and who says "possum" knows how to catch possums; and he will bring some home. Blessed is the man who knows where to borrow brains.

The door to the room of success always swings on the hinges of opposition. Did you ever drive down a country road and see an old farmhouse with no windows and no doors and with nobody living in it? Do you know why it was left open like that?—because there was nothing in there that anybody wanted. The more valuable the treasures in a house, the harder it is to get into that house. You would have a hard time breaking into a bank in this city. Something that is worth having is in there. Money, something that jingles in pockets that folks like to hear—something that used to buy groceries before we had so many points!—is there.

I saw the crown jewels in London. I would like to see you get them. You would have to go through the army, through guards, and break down doors that are locked and barred. People think those jewels are valuable. They are valuable stuff. They are hard to get.

Young people, the door to the room of success was hung on the hinges of opposition by Almighty God. God wants you to appreciate values. He says, "This thing is worth something, go through the door and get it." You say, "The door is hard to open." God says, "I know it! I am the One who made the door and hung it on its hinges. If you don't want to go in, go on about your business."

Sometimes people say about a student, "He learns without studying." That isn't really so. He may be learning a few facts, but he is not learning how to build character. I have heard people say of others, "They do it without an effort." That isn't so. No man ever did worth-while things without effort.

Did you ever read about a hunchbacked painter who lay flat on his back and painted pictures that the world goes to see? I suppose you have if you know anything about art.

Did you ever see a beautiful floral garden? The flowers didn't just bloom. Somebody cultivated them and cared for them. And the flowers of character will not bloom long in your life unless you are willing to make an effort. God will let the thorns kill the flowers if you don't cultivate them.

When gratitude dies on the altar of a man's heart, that man is well-nigh hopeless. As long as folks have a sense of gratitude, there is hope for them. If you are a preacher-boy decent enough to write a letter to the woman who cooked you a good dinner and say in it, "You were very nice to cook that good dinner. I am sorry you went to so much trouble, but how I do appreciate your kindness to me. I hope some day to let you know just how much I appreciate all you did for me." —there is some hope for you.

A young preacher who will go out to a home and let a sweet, tired country mother tug and toil to cook his food; see her sit down at the table, take her apron, and wipe the sweat from her brow after she has worked for him; and then not be decent enough to write a letter when he goes away has nothing to him. He is a dirty, lousy scoundrel! You don't have to be told to say "thank you" if there is anything to you; you will do it spontaneously.

I wonder if there is a student here this morning who has never been decent enough to write his mother a love letter and tell her how sweet she has been to him. Do you write your dad letters and thank him for tugging and toiling to send you to school? If you do, there is something to you.

There are students here, maybe, who never thanked a teacher for extra attention. Jesus said, "Where are the nine?" One out of ten had enough to him to say, "Thank you." I'll venture that fellow turned out well. I'll venture the assertion that those lazy, dirty loafers whom Jesus Christ healed and who didn't thank Him had to have somebody take care of them the rest of their lives. I'll venture that the one who thanked Jesus, said, "I have to run home and kiss my mother and see my folks. Thank you, Jesus." I would have given him a job had I lived in that country. I would have let those other dirty ingrates tough it out the best they could.

Most of the students who have gone out from Bob Jones College are appreciative of all we have done for them. Many write wonderful letters expressing their gratitude. A few students who owe practically everything they are on earth to the college have gone out disloyal and critical. Some have called me a dictator because I would not lower the standards and compromise the principles on which the college was founded.

One time a man mistreated me. I knew he mistreated me. I told him he mistreated me. A few years later he did for me one of the greatest favors ever done for me by anybody on this earth. I saw him one day. He said, "Dr. Bob, don't hold that thing I did to you one time against me." "Oh," I said, "my friend, how could I hold anything against you? You have done for me such a great favor—the water of this kindness washes away all the old mud that was there before." Young people, if there happens to be a little flower of gratitude left in your soul, take care of that flower!

It is a sin for any man to do less than his best. As I have preached up and down this country I have had people ask me what sin is. I could give a lot of theological definitions and discuss them, but I will tell you what sin is. Sin is anything in your life that keeps you from hitting the bull's eye when you shoot for God. Is it a long tongue? Is it a "gripe-y" disposition? Is it the disease of too much love? Is it laziness? Anything in your life that keeps you from making the best record possible in college this semester is a sin, even though it might be a date with a nice girl. Your business is to make during this semester the best record it is possible for you to make. Anything short of that is a sin.

The measure of your responsibility is the measure of your opportunity. The sort of opportunity you have determines your responsibility. You have a good chance. You are in a Christian college. You have academic privileges. You have high scholastic standards. You are in an atmosphere of culture where there is an open Bible, where there are praying friends. The measure of your responsibility is the measure of your opportunity.

Pride is the stone over which most people stumble. I have come down the road of life and found people all around me who have fallen. Most of them stumbled over the stone of pride. "Pride goeth before destruction, and an haughty spirit before a fall." That is what God said about it. The higher a bird flies, the farther he has to come down to get a worm when he is hungry. Don't fly too high, for you are going to get hungry some day—you are going to need a worm.

Do you know why you get so upset when somebody corrects you? It is your old, rotten pride. Watch out for the stumbling-stone of pride. I told you that on the highway of life God has put stones in your path and that He wants you to make not stumbling-stones but stepping-stones out of them. But God never put the stone of pride in your way. That is the devil's stone. By the grace of God, though, you can step on that one, too. When you step on it, mash it flat; crush it! It is a dangerous stone. Watch out for it!

Prayer: "Heavenly Father, we call Thee to witness today to the desire of our hearts to do everything that it is possible for us to do for these Christian young people in this Christian college. We do not want the devil's crowd to get along better in this world than we do. We are Christians. We have Thee back of us. Everything else being equal, we ought to outrun the other crowd on the road of success. We shouldn't come behind men of the world. We remember, our Father, that Jesus said, 'The children of this world are in their generation wiser than the children of light.' We are the children of light if we are saved by Thy grace. We ought to be wiser than these supposedly successful people in the world. They are not really successful if they haven't God. But even in the things which men call success we ought, by Thy grace, to excel. So give us Thy grace. There are people in this student body, many of them lovely young people, who need to get under conviction. They haven't measured up to the high standards of God, and they know it. Give them Thy power and Thy blessing today. Give them the grace they need and the stiffening of backbone, the determination, the will power, and character to go through with God. We ask it in the name of Jesus Christ our Lord. Amen."

Things I Have Learned

No. 3

FOR the last several mornings I have been trying to bring to you some of the practical Christian philosophy which I have learned along life's way. I am going to try to crowd into the next few minutes a good many things; so I can mention them only briefly.

The men who move this world along right lines believe in an ever-present, real God. They don't talk about "a first great cause." If you are going places in this world and doing good in this world, you must believe in an ever-present God. Always God has been real to the people I have known who were really worth while.

"Simplicity is truth's most becoming garb." Great people are always simple people. Big people don't strut. Little people strut. I saw a man one time who was small of stature. He was the worst strutter I ever saw. He would throw his shoulders back and put his chest out and talk about knocking somebody's head off. One day I said to him, "Why do you act like that?" He said, "I have to act like that to make myself feel I am as big as other men."

Did you ever see a bulldog go down the street? Did you notice how steadily he walked? A little "fyst" comes down the street barking and making a noise, strutting his stuff. The bulldog goes on about his business. If you are real and are going down the way of life with real character, you don't have to strut. Don't strut! Don't "put on the dog"! Just be yourself. God never made another person like you. How wonderfully good He was to not make anybody else like you! Suppose the world were filled with people like you!

Sometimes I thank God that, in a way, I had to grow up alone. I never associated with any evangelists. I never saw Sam Jones. I never saw Dwight L. Moody. I was brought up in the country all alone. I had to be myself. I had to make my own sermons, do my own preaching. Of course, I might have preached better had I preached somebody else's sermons, but I preached my own sermons and had my own style. I am glad as I look back now that I did.

Beware of the man who "kowtows" to his superiors or who is rude to his inferiors. Watch the fellow who is always "boot-licking" the person who is above him and always looking with contempt on the person beneath him. Great people do not bow down to or "kowtow" to anybody. They respect men. They honor great men. But they don't "kowtow" to them. Great people are always kind to their inferiors. Always! You show me a fellow who is hard-boiled and mean to a fellow under him, and I will show you a fellow who has nothing to his character. Watch that kind of man.

Beware of unreasonable people. Good men are always reasonable men. When you find a man with whom you cannot reason, something is wrong with that man.

A little country schoolboy caught a bumblebee one time, put it in a little tin box, and put the box in his hip pocket. He went to the classroom. After a while the lid got off the box. The bumblebee began to operate back in that section of the country and the boy began to wiggle. The teacher said, "Sit still, Johnny." Johnny said, "All right." The teacher said again, "Johnny, sit still." He said, "All right, teacher!" "Johnny! sit still!" He said, "All right." *"Johnny! Didn't I tell you to sit still!"* "Yes, but there is something going on back here you don't know nothing about!" Johnny replied.

Listen, when you find a person who takes an unreasonable position, there is something stinging him. You may not know what is stinging him, but something is wrong with him. When a student in this college gets wrong, gets off-pitch spiritually, he immediately becomes unreasonable. The Bible says the prodigal son "came to himself." There is a form of insanity brought about by wrongdoing.

Young folks who play a loose moral game are always losing even though they may seem to be winning. If there is a just God on the throne of this universe, the man who does right is bound to win sometime, somewhere. The man who does wrong is bound to lose sometime, somewhere. God Almighty has stacked the cards of the universe against wrongdoing. God Almighty fixed your body so you couldn't beat the game of sin. God made your brain so you couldn't do wrong and get away with it. The folks who play loose, play to lose.

God sometimes uses a man who never had a chance, but God never uses a man who had a chance and, wouldn't take it or who could make a chance and wouldn't do it. I remember a man who was one time holding a revival meeting in East Tennessee. This man, a converted "jailbird," stood up and said, "I thank God I never had a college education." I read the other day where the man was in trouble again. When he first started to preach, some people thought he was going to turn the earth upside down. I knew he would fail. I wouldn't boast if I hadn't had opportunities. I wish I could have had the chance you students have. I might have been somebody. Beware of the men who glory in the fact that they never had a chance.

A fellow came to see me a few years ago and asked me to help him buy an automobile and a loud-speaker so he could conduct street services. He was a young man just over twenty years of age, maybe twenty-four or twenty-five. He talked with me fifteen minutes, and I think I have never heard a man in so short a time make as many mistakes in grammar as he did. I asked him how long he had been a Christian. He told me he had been a Christian ten years. I asked him if he were in high school when he was converted. He said he had just started to high school and quit. He said he had been married a few years, was married before he was twenty. I said, "I wouldn't give you a cent. You are a disgrace to the ministry." He said, "What do you mean?" I said, "You have no right to stand on the street corner and through a loudspeaker give the Gospel in as poor English as you use. In thirty days' time you could get over some of that poor

English." He could have got an instructor in English and in thirty days been cured of some of his mistakes. I have no respect for a lazy loafer who talks about loving God and serving God but who won't even study. A lazy preacher! A lazy missionary! A lazy school teacher! I have seen God use men who never had an opportunity, but I have never seen God use a man long who could make an opportunity and wouldn't do it.

There is only one thing to do about anything, and that is to do the right thing. When you come to where the road parts, stop long enough to ask just this one question and answer it: "Which is the right road?" Don't ask anything else. And when you ask that question and answer that question and decide in the presence of God which is the right road, just go down that road. Just do right! Do right if the stars fall. Do right if there are a million guns mounted upon hell's battlements turned loose on you. *Just do right!*

The God who made the law of addition can beat anybody in the world adding. My Lord said, "Seek ye first the kingdom of God, and his righteousness; and all these things shall be added unto you." If you will put first things first, the God who made the laws of addition and subtraction and multiplication—that God who can beat all mathematicians adding—will add to your life what you need. A girl said to me one time, "I think I will quit school. I have a job that will pay good money." Say, did you come to college just to get a job to make money? If you did, you are not a Bob Jones College type student.

Some day you may be an old woman with false teeth and dim eyes, sitting in a corner somewhere. Old Father Time may have pinched your face full of wrinkles. What are you going to have then? God will add to you then things that are better than money. An old man said to me one time, "When I get lonely I quote the Psalms and the great classic poems; I go over in my mind something that Tennyson said. God adds in a great many ways—not just bread and butter and clothes. God adds light and happiness and peace and contentment and stimulation.

Every dissipation of youth has to be paid for with a draft on old age. You can stay up all night now. Young folks can dance, drink, carouse, and then sleep it off. But pay day comes some day. You will draw a draft on old age, if you ever get there, to pay for the dissipation of youth. No man ever is the same after he has sinned. Somebody said, "Sam Jones was a great preacher because he had a bad past." He was a great preacher in spite of his bad past. Sin always leaves you worse than it finds you.

This is not the age of the thinker. It is the age of the doer. As education has increased, thinking has decreased. If you are going to think today you will not move in a big circle. Most people are not thinking. I was in New York one day. A fellow started across Broadway and an automobile ran over him and killed him. We gathered around him. Somebody said, "Poor fellow, he wasn't thinking." I said, "He was thinking. That is the reason he got killed." You go to thinking while crossing a street and some fool will run over you. Don't try to think on a public highway. But I would advise you to once in a while sit down alone and do a little thinking.

It is at the Cross that we get the power to live the Sermon on the Mount. It is not Christ in a manger, but Christ on the cross dying for me. These preachers who talk about the Sermon on the Mount and say, "I'm for the Sermon on the Mount," never live the Sermon on the Mount if they reject the blood of Jesus Christ. I suggest that you once in a while sing the old song, "What can wash away my sin? Nothing but the blood of Jesus."

The greatest ability is dependability. As I have gone along the way of life I have met a great many people who said, "I haven't any ability." I have always told them that they didn't have to have any ability—that God has enough for both of them. The greatest ability anybody needs, the average man can have. The greatest ability is dependability; and the greatest ability on earth, the humblest student in this college can have. Learn to be dependable.

God and one man make a majority in any community. Never mind the crowd against you. Be sure God is for you. Don't worry. Learn to stand alone. Say, listen! if you can't be the only one who walks out of a meeting, you are not much anyhow. Did you ever have to stand up and say, "Ladies and gentlemen, excuse me. I can't stay in this meeting. This is not my atmosphere and my place. I wish to be courteous, but I am a Christian"? Did you ever go to a place where everybody lighted a cigarette except you and where people looked at you and wondered? Did you ever sit down at a table where everybody was sipping wine and you had to turn your glass up in order to be a nice, decent, Christian gentleman or lady? You don't have to be queer. Just be decent. The man who is decent always seems queer to the fellow who isn't decent.

One time a man was going home at Christmas time.

He was drunk. As he dragged along the street he saw another man coming along with a sack of flour on his shoulder.   The drunken man stopped a third man and said, "Mister, am I seeing right?" The man said, "I suppose so, what do you mean?" The drunk man said, "Is that a sack of flour that fellow has on his shoulder?" The man said, "Yes, that is a sack of flour on his shoulder." "Well, am I right about it being Christmas time?" "Yes, it is Christmas time," the man said. "It is Christmas time and he is going home with a sack of flour on his shoulder—I'll bet the fool hasn't a bit of liquor in his house!" the drunkard exclaimed. A laboring man with an honest heart going home with a sack of flour on his shoulder seemed queer to a drunkard.

There is a way to test your character. Would you like to be able to know what kind of person you are? I will tell you how to find out. Sometime today go to your room and get everybody out for a little while. Get alone. Shut the door. Put a chair out in front of you. Put yourself in that chair. Back off and look yourself in the eye and ask yourself this question, "What would you do if you knew nobody would ever know it?" That is what you are!

Would you cheat on examination if you knew positively that nobody on earth or in eternity would ever know it? If you would, then you are a cheat. Men are not liars because they lie; they lie because they are liars.   Men are not thieves because they steal; they steal because they are thieves. Stealing doesn't make you a thief; being a thief makes you steal. Men are not cheats because they cheat; they cheat because they are cheats. Men are not sinners because they sin; they sin because they are sinners.

What you would do if nobody but God Almighty ever knew it is exactly what you are. Don't fool yourself. Don't kid yourself along. Say, this is turning the light on, isn't it? This is enough to make all of us go to the mourner's bench. This is enough to make everybody in this house say, "God be merciful to me a sinner." I ask you this morning at the beginning of a new semester this question: What are you in the sight of God?

One time a man was going through a cathedral in Europe. He heard a noise high in the dome. He said, "Who is up there?" A fellow said, "I'm up here." The man below said, "What are you doing up there?" He said, "I'm painting this dome." The man below said, "Nobody can see it." The man above answered, "Nobody but God and me."

God knows. He sees you. And you can't pop a sham life off on Him. What are you in the sight of God?

Prayer: "Our Heavenly Father, help these young people, most of whom have high ambitions and holy purposes, to draw upon the infinite resources of divine grace to be all they ought to be. Help us to know that anything short of our best is sin. Help each one of us this morning while our heads are bowed to say, 'By the grace of God I will do my very best to be everything God would have me be.' We thank Thee that we can do anything Thou wouldst have us do— travel any road that Thou wouldst have us travel, climb any mountain that Thou wouldst have us climb, scale any wall that Thou wouldst have us scale, cross any stream that Thou wouldst have us cross. Help us to go through with God. As we get down to the routine of this second semester beginning today, help us to write a clean record on a clean page. When we come to the close of this semester, may we not look back with bitter memories to soiled and stained pages. If there is one student in Bob Jones College who isn't right with God, help such an one this morning while our heads are bowed to say, 'God be merciful to me a sinner.' Help us to know that God is our Friend, that He is ever present with us, able to take care of us, able to succor us when we are tempted, able to keep us from falling. Help us to know that some day the Lord Jesus Christ will present us faultless in the presence of His glory. Keep us true to Thy Son and our Saviour this day and every day this semester, we beg in the ever wonderful name of Jesus Christ our Lord. Amen."

Things I Have Learned

No. 4

I WANT to speak to you again this morning about some lessons that I have learned along life's way. *A man can do anything he ought to do.* If you ought to do a thing, you can do it. People say to me, "I don't think that is correct. I ought to do so and so, but I can't." Well, if you can't, you ought not to. I have found that there is always a way to do the thing that I should do. It may be difficult. God doesn't always take us over smooth roads. It isn't good for a horse always to travel a level road. I learned when I was a boy that a horse could hold up longer if there were some grades in the road. When a horse goes uphill he exercises certain muscles. When he goes downhill he exercises some other muscles. On a level road the horse exercises the same muscles all the time.

You needn't expect an easy way in life. Life's road is never easy. If you haven't any difficulties, that very fact makes difficulties for you. A level, smooth road with no grades to go up is the most difficult road leading to the place we call success.

You can do anything you ought to do. I said that one time to a boy who said he ought to go to college but couldn't. Listen, any boy who ought to go to college *can* go. Any young person who ought to stay in college can stay in college. Anybody who ought to go to China as a missionary, can go to China.

A girl said, "I was called to China as a missionary but I couldn't get there." God never called a girl to go to China who couldn't get to China. If she couldn't go, she wasn't called. God is not that kind of God. God doesn't call you to be a missionary and never open a missionary door to you or give you a key to open a missionary door. People sometimes want God to unlock the door for them when they can unlock it themselves. God won't unlock the door for you if you have in your pocket a key to the door. Go unlock the door yourself! Some people are always asking God to send them money when they could get it themselves. They are too lazy to go out and get it. They want God to be a waiting boy and bring it to them. God won't send you money if you have two hands with which to work, two eyes with which to see, and two legs on which to go and find it. You needn't sit down and ask God to send it to you. Ask God to send you out to get it. You can do anything you ought to do.

It is a man's duty to go as far as he can on the right road. Don't ever wonder where you are going to come out. Just wonder if you are on the right road. I ask but one question about anything. I never ask where the road is leading. I just ask if it is the right road. If a road is the right road, it will lead out at the right place. Just go as far as you can on the right road. If you will go as far as you can, you can always go farther. The children of Israel came to a sea. That was as far as they could go, but they went as far as that.

When they got to the sea God reached down out of Heaven with the hand of His power, pushed the water back, and said, "Go on."

If you will go as far as you can on the right road, then when you get to a sea God Almighty will divide the waters for you. When you get to a wall that you can't scale, God will tear down the wall or put up against the wall a ladder of power. When you get to a mountain you can't climb, God will drop a little rope down from the mountain-top and say, "Take hold; I will pull you up." Keep going. Don't wonder where you are coming out. The right road always leads out at the right place. Go as far as you can on the right road.

Back of God's commands He puts His omnipotence. God never told a man to go forward without giving him a little push so he could go forward. God never told a man how to live without giving him power to live just as He told him to live. When God says, "Forward march!" God equips you to march. I have found that God always pushes you with an omnipotent hand down the road if you listen to His command. That is the difference between our Christian religion and the religions of the world. The religions of the world tell people what to do and leave them helpless to do it. God is different. He tells people what to do and gives them power to do it. That is the glory of our Christianity. God tells us how to live right. He gives us the orders, the commands; then He imparts to us the power to carry out those commands. Back of His commands He puts His omnipotence.

Do not sacrifice the permanent on the altar of the immediate. Many young people think in terms of today and not in terms of tomorrow. You had better be a little hungry today and have food in the future. You had better wear poor clothes now and have a warm coat when you get old. You will need a warm coat in your old age more than you do when you are young. So many young people in this world are sacrificing all the future on the altar of the immediate. They are fools to do it. That is the explanation of many things that are happening today. What do you think is going to happen to the girls who are hanging around these cocktail lounges and bars with a cocktail glass in one hand and a cigarette in the other? What do you think is going to happen to the young people who are playing the game loose in this country—the young folks who are living sensual, superficial, unclean lives? They are locking skeletons in the closets of their lives, and the bones of those skeletons will rattle in their ears in coming years. You just can't get away with sin. Let me tell you something—you may get by the teacher today; but you can't get by life twenty-five years from now. Don't sacrifice the permanent on the altar of the immediate!

Figure on the worst but hope for the best. Don't ever figure on the best. I never do. Every year before we open college the business manager, Bob, Jr., and I talk things over. We figure the minimum income and the maximum outgo. We never figure the maximum income. We figure the minimum income. The business manager says, "Well, we should have so much a month this year and we shall probably have to spend on an average so much a month." I say, "Now, let's think this over just a little. Don't you think we had better cut down that income? Something might happen. An epidemic might come. A building might burn. Something might disturb our plans. Cut down your income. Add to your outgo. Figure on the worst, but hope for the best."

A wise general out to win a battle always figures that the first lines may not hold. He figures the second may not hold, and the third may not hold, and so on. He figures on the worst and hopes for the best. That is good sense.

A person said to me one time, "I don't believe there is a hell." I figure there is a hell. That is the worst thing I can figure on. Suppose I find there is no hell? Suppose I go out into eternity and ask, "Where is it?" Suppose somebody answers, "Where is what?" "Why," I say, "where is that place I used to hear about—the place where 'the fire is never quenched and the worm never dies'? Where is it?" The person answers me, "There is no such place out here." "There isn't?" "No, there is no such place."

If that happened I would be as well off as anybody else. I would like to know who would be better off in eternity than I if there is no hell. But suppose there is a hell and a fool doesn't figure on it. He might get in it! I figure on the worst and hope for the best. That is good sense for time and for eternity.

You cannot do wrong and get away with it. The game of sin is an unbeatable game! I have learned that the wisest man who ever lived on earth, the greatest genius who ever breathed, was not mighty enough to do wrong and get away with it. No student in Bob Jones College ever did wrong and got away with it. Oh, it may be that a student didn't get caught in just the thing he did; but he got caught in his character.

The worst thing that can happen to a student is to break a rule and not get caught. It will mar him and hurt him in coming years a thousand times worse than it would hurt him to get caught now.

Listen, you are no friend to your roommate when you cover up for him or for her the violation of rules. The worst enemy you have is a girl or boy who covers up your wrongdoing and lets you get away with the breach of a rule or regulation here. I have known students whose lives were cursed by that sort of process. I have heard students say, "Oh, I wouldn't squeal on a friend." Don't call yourself a friend if you say that. If you are a friend to your roommate you say to that roommate, "We are living in a Christian college. There are rules and regulations here. They were made by both students and faculty, and we signed them. We promised to keep them. I won't cover up for a criminal!" Listen! Every great criminal in this world was a little criminal one time. He began with a little breach of law, a trampling under foot of rules. That is the way he started, then there came a time of calamity and sorrow. You can't do wrong and get away with it.

You girls, you Christian girls, let me tell you something: the girls out in the world living their superficial lives may think you are wallflowers at the party because you are decent. You hold your head up and tell them that you have too much sense to play the game loose as they are playing it. I was laughed at when I was a boy for being decent. Some of those who laughed at me wound up in jail. Some of them are in suicides' graves. Some of them are in hell! You shoot straight! God Almighty organized this universe against wrongdoing. He organized the universe to work in harmony with right living. You can't beat the game of sin!

If you will give God your heart He will "comb the kinks out of your head." God doesn't ask you for your head. What would He want with it? There isn't anything in there anyhow! Say, what does God who is infinite in wisdom want with your little, puny finite brain? God Almighty wants your heart!

Suppose your girl said, "I will give you my brains." You want the heart of your girl, not just her head. Suppose you tell your mother, "I will give you my brain, Mother, but not the affections of a child's heart." God is called a Father. God is spoken of as One who comforts as a mother comforts. God wants love and affection. Your little, puny head doesn't mean anything to God. People say, "I just can't believe." They are liars. People used to fool me that way. People say, "He is an honest doubter." He isn't an honest doubter; he is either an egotist, or he has some gross sin in his life. Every man who struts around saying that he is an honest doubter is either living in gross immorality or is an egomaniac, I don't care how humble he talks. Jesus Christ fixed that forever when He said, "If any man will do His will, he shall know of the doctrine." *Jesus Christ never lets any man live in intellectual doubt who in his heart honestly wants to know the truth.*

The world isn't filled with skeptics; it is filled with sinners with dirty hearts. I have seen atheists converted in a moment of time. All doubts were dissolved like mist before the morning sun. People say, "I have intellectual problems." Oh, you egotistical upstart! You have a heart problem—a heart in rebellion against

the commandments of God and the authority of **God!**
Get your heart right and you won't have trouble with
your head.

When in doubt, play safe. Years ago in New York
City I saw an old preacher coming down the street.
He was a handsome old fellow. He wore a cutaway
coat, gray trousers, well-shined shoes, and a silk hat.
When a person saw him coming down the street he
knew somebody was coming.

I wonder when you walk into a room if people say,
"Somebody has come," or do they just say, "*It* is here
again." It is nice to look at a man and know he is a
man—not just a pair of pants, not just a coat and
collar and tie—but a man!

This man looked liked a man, walked like a man!
I had seen him before and knew him fairly well. We
stopped on Broadway, shook hands, and had a nice
visit. In the course of conversation he said, "Brother
Bob, weren't you reared down in Alabama?" I said,
"Yes, Sir." He said, "I was, too. That is my home
state. I was born in Alabama." Then he told me the
following story:

"When I was a boy just twenty years old I lived in
a certain little town. The first job I ever had in my
life was a job as ticket agent, telegraph operator, and
depot agent there at that little railroad station. The
job paid me thirty dollars a month. That was good
money in those days for a young fellow twenty years
old. It didn't cost much to live.

"I was in love with a beautiful girl. Oh, it was wonderful! She was just eighteen years old. She had
wonderful eyes and hair as black as a slice out of midnight. Oh, she was lovely, lovely, *lovely!*"

The old fellow kept talking and waxing more elo-
quent. A strange emotional note was in his throat. I
found myself saying,

"Backward, turn backward, O Time, in your flight,
Give me a chance again just for tonight!"

I just can't help being interested in the love affairs
of young people. I get disgusted with some of them.
I can't have much respect for a girl or boy who will
pair off in college and never know there is anybody
in school except themselves. If I were a boy in this
college I wouldn't let any frizzly-headed girl tie me
down to just one. I don't believe it is wholesome for
any boy in college to go with the same girl all the
time. When I was a boy in college we all, of course,
had our own special girls; but we had friends, too. We
went with girls who had enough confidence in us, and
who had enough common sense to want us to have
friends. We used to see to it that all the girls had
dates, too. We checked all of them in. When I was
a boy young people acted like gentlemen and ladies.
I can't help getting disgusted with a little senseless girl
and a good-for-nothing boy who go "blooming crazy"
about each other. I don't like these girls and boys
who stand around and look as if they could eat each
other up. Some day they will be sorry they didn't!
If you can be in love and still use good sense, you
are somebody. One of the greatest tests of your character is your ability to be sensible when you are in
love. I salute every student in Bob Jones College this
morning who loves somebody and still uses good sense.
I wouldn't be an idiot. If I had somebody in love with

me who was an idiot, I would check the idiot off my list. I wouldn't want to marry an idiot. It takes real character to live with somebody who has good sense. If you get tied up with an idiot, you surely will be up against it. But I can't help being interested in the love affairs of young people. I make dates for them here sometimes. If any of you girls or boys need help, ask the young people at my table if I can't make dates for them.

Well, this old gentleman went on with his story. He said, "The first day I worked at my job I thought about my girl all day. As I said, I was twenty years old and was making thirty dollars a month. I decided I would go to see her and propose to her that night. It was a wonderful night. The moon was shining."

Say, by the way, it is a little dangerous to make love on a moonlight night, or on the seashore, or in the springtime with flowers about you. You don't know exactly whether it is the romance of the occasion or whether it is love. If I were a girl I think I would take my sweetheart to the middle of the desert. I would wait until the sweat was rolling off my face. I would look at him when he was panting for breath and say, "Do you love me *now?*" The average boy with any sort of a romantic nature will make love on a moonlight night.

"So," he said, "we stood there on the porch. It was a lovely night. The moonlight got tangled in her hair, and, oh, those marvelous eyes! She told me she would marry me. I went home so happy I didn't sleep all night.

"The next morning bright and early I went to the depot and sat down. In a little while a message came over the wire, click, click, click—'Thirty-seven, thirty-eight pass; sidetrack thirty-seven, let thirty-eight through.' There was a single track with a little switch in front of the station. I had to let one of the trains stop so the other one could go through. I should have written down the instructions, but I didn't. I said, 'I will just remember it,' and kept thinking about my girl. Fifteen minutes went by. I heard thirty-seven blow in one direction and thirty-eight blow in another direction. The trains were coming like lightning. One of them had to go on the sidetrack and I had forgotten which one. I was in an awful fix; so I just pulled the old switch and shut both trains out. I went out and said to one engineer, 'Come on the sidetrack,' and to the other one, 'Go on through.' But I hadn't much more than given the instructions until I remembered I had put the wrong train on the sidetrack and I was in trouble. But I had made up my mind to be truthful and honest."

Listen to me, young people, you never get out of a hole by lying. A lie will dig the hole deeper. Truth will not always get you out of a hole, but lying will *never* do it. When you get in a hole, put up a ladder of truth and try to climb out. Don't lie; don't be a humbug; don't be a fourflusher! Listen, it is not only wrong to lie, but also it doesn't pay to lie. There is something about telling the truth that disarms even your enemies. You can't lie yourself to success. You can travel the road of truth. So travel it!

This old gentleman said: "I sat down and wrote headquarters. I told them exactly what happened. I told them I didn't write down the instructions, asked them please to forgive me and told them I would never again fail to write down orders that came over the wire. I told them I wasn't quite myself anyhow, that I had not slept all night. I told them I had become engaged the night before and that if they fired me they would break the heart of the finest girl in the world and would ruin me. I asked them to please give me a chance. A few days later I got a letter back. My hands were shaking so I could hardly open it, but I opened it and read something like this:

> " 'My dear young Fellow:
>
> " 'We are sorry you didn't write down the instructions that came over the wire. The rule is: 'Write down all orders.' We are sorry you didn't obey orders. We are glad, however, that you are truthful and that when the emergency came you knew how to meet it. Because when in doubt you played safe we are going to promote you. We are going to give you a good job so you can get married right away.' "

When in doubt, play safe. If somebody says to you, "Let's go to such and such a place," and you say, "I uon't know whether I ought to go," then don't go! If somebody says, "Let's do so-and-so," and you are not sure whether you should do it, don't do it! When in doubt, play safe! You can't miss out this way.

You never wondered whether snow on a mountaintop was white. When you wonder whether snow is dirty, it is dirty. You never heard anybody say, "What is the harm in going to prayer meeting?" You never heard anybody say around Bob Jones College, "Do you suppose it would be wrong if I read a chapter out of the Bible before I go to sleep?" If you ask what is wrong with a thing, there is usually something wrong with it.

One morning a man was standing near a window. His wife said, "Put that collar on and come on to breakfast." He said, "I am just trying to decide whether it is dirty." She said, "If it is doubtful, it is dirty!" Boys and girls, if it is doubtful, it is wrong.

Prayer: "Our Father, bless us as we go to our classes. Help us to play the game of life honorably so we can play it successfully. Help us to know we can't beat the game of sin. Help us to know that God is a practical God and the Bible is a practical book and Christianity is a practical Christianity and the Christian philosophy is a practical philosophy. Help us to go straight. Help us to trust God so we can live right. Impart to us the power to obey Thy commands. Keep us faithful to Thee. In Jesus' name we pray. Amen."

Obedience Necessary

I WANT to talk to you out of my heart this morning, and I want you to think while I talk. I have a message that I want to get over to all of you, both students and members of the faculty.

I want to talk to you about the purpose of this institution—the main, underlying purpose back of Bob Jones College. I wonder if you know what we are trying to do. Do you know what we are up to here? Well, I'll tell you what we are trying to do. We are trying to train Christian leaders for a chaotic world. I want to get the idea over to you, so you will understand the philosophy and also understand the approach of this institution.

Yes, we are endeavoring to train Christian leaders for a chaotic world. There has been a dearth of leadership in the world for a long time, not only Christian leadership but also all other kinds of leadership. Do you know why there are dictators in Europe? Because most of the people in Europe are just ordinary. They are just so ordinary. Did you know that Mussolini, as mean as he is, went to his position by prison and sacrifice? Did you know that that little paper hanger in Germany, as low-down and devilish as he is, knew the lesson of obedience, knew what it meant to face hardships? Did you know that up in Russia, Stalin suffered to get where he is? The reason we have dictators in Europe is that the masses of the people have little character. They will follow any man who has anything to him, whether he is right or wrong.

We have also come to bad days in America. The Democratic Party seems to have just one man big enough to be President. The Republican Party a few years ago at a National Convention agreed upon and nominated just one man as a candidate for the presidency. Nobody else got in on the thing at all. Now, that is a bad situation. That is the way it is all over this country. I can count on the fingers of my hands the great, outstanding preachers of America. There are only a few great doctors and a few great lawyers. The whole educational world is chaotic. The leadership in the educational world is in a terrible state. This country is filled with wrecked colleges. The business world is alive now only because of a peculiar mechanical stimulation it is getting from Washington. The business world is chaotic. And the Christian world is the same way.

Now, Bob Jones College is trying its best to produce Christian leaders who will be able to stand up under chaotic conditions and be worth-while in our modern world. I want you to understand that this morning. We are not trying to produce great scholars. We hope to discover a few young people with scholastic possibilities. There are not many great scholars in this country. In the scientific world there are a few outstanding men. In the literary world there are only a few great men. You can count very easily the great scholars of the country, *the great scholars.* There are not many of them. We, of course, are trying to raise the scholastic level as high as possible and we are hoping to find somebody in Bob Jones College who may have great scholastic possibilities; but primarily we are not trying to produce great scholars. We are trying here to produce great Christian leaders. The world needs Christian leadership. And when this war is over it is going to need Christian leadership more than ever.

Listen to me, I want you young people who are here in this institution— especially you who may have come here to Bob Jones College just to go to college—to know what we are up to so you can go along with us if you have anything to you. We want you, when you finish at Bob Jones College, to go back to your community a leader, a Christian leader. We want you to have the elements of leadership.

We have studied this business of leadership. It is very interesting. There is one essential thing in producing great leaders and that is *obedience.*

Some weeks ago I was in New York City. On Broadway just diagonally across from the hotel where I stayed, there is a picture house. It is not a theatrical place. It is simply a place where people see the newsreels. Of course, we are against the whole commercial theatrical set-up. I went in there because I was interested in seeing war pictures. I saw a picture that I wish every one of you could see, that is, if you have enough sense to appreciate it. Here is the story:

Men to be trained for special leadership in our military organization are selected from all over the country and taken down to Florida. You never in your life saw anything like what they have done to them while they are in training. I sat there and said, "O boy, I wish I had that kind of power in Bob Jones College!" Those men walked in there, and I never before saw such obedience. Middle-aged men, formerly prominent in the business and professional world, had officers stick their noses right in their faces and give them such orders as you never heard in your life. Those officers are interested in producing men who will have leadership ability and be worth something, men who can direct other men, men who can lead our forces to battle and to victory. Do you know what they do? They throw out over half of them. Hundreds go there, but only a certain percentage are found capable of going ahead with the training that is necessary to make leaders.

Listen, if at the end of ninety days only half of you were left, you would be doing pretty well in comparison with what the army does in training its leaders. Suppose we have to cast out fifty per cent of you. Suppose we have to say to many of you, "You are worthless as a leader. Just go on back home. It is all right; you be a follower. You will never be a leader."

Those training men for leadership in the military world say, and it is right in line with what the Bible teaches, that *all leaders have to learn to obey.* The fundamental thing, the essential thing, in training for leadership is to learn obedience. If you can't "take it on the chin," if you can't obey, you will never be a leader. I wouldn't have anybody at Bob Jones College —if you were so old your nose and chin met and you had to spit out of the side of your mouth—I wouldn't have you if you couldn't obey!

Some fellow says, "I don't want anybody telling me when to get up in the morning." I've got two or three boys here I am waiting for "Uncle Sam" to get. I talked to one this morning. If they put him in a camp a thousand miles from this place I think I'll go to see him. I want to walk in there and look at that "guy." I want to see him "get up in the morning." "Uncle Sam" may put him in the jungles of some island in the Pacific. I don't want the Japs to shoot him, because he is a nice boy. I want the snakes to hiss at him. I don't want them to bite him! I just want them to hiss at him. I want the mosquitoes to bite him. I hope they won't have malaria. I want him to be thirsty for a little while when he can't get a drink of water. It would do him good! He would say, "Mama, Mama; I want some water!" But "mama" couldn't wait on him there.

Listen, did you know, did you know—listen! even the devil himself has to take over God's philosophy to make a soldier. The devil can't make a soldier with his own philosophy. The devil's philosophy is "Do as you please." God's philosophy is "Do what you are told to do." The devil can't make a soldier without using God's philosophy to do it.

You can't be a success in the business world without using God's philosophy. There are only two philosophies—the devil's philosophy and God's philosophy. The devil's philosophy is "Do as you please," and God's philosophy is "Do what you are told to do—*do right!*"

In the Old Testament we are told that Samuel raised this question: "Hath the Lord as great delight in burnt-offerings and sacrifices as in obeying the voice of the Lord? Behold *to obey is better than sacrifice.*" If there had been no disobedience, sacrifice would never have been necessary. "By one man's disobedience many were made sinners." If there had been no disobedience, there would have been no cross, no tragedy, no blood. Disobedience damned the human race. It is better to do what God says and not have to repent, than it is to disobey God and have to repent. Sin never did pay. It never will pay!

Every year about this time the little fellows begin to show up. Some folks come here who were sort of the "cock of the walk" at home. We don't have any "cocks of the walk" around this place. We all walk along together. Some of you want to get in a little crowd where people will think you are somebody. Some of you can't be anything big if you are in a big crowd; so you want to get in a little crowd where people will know you are around.

When I was in college a fellow came to the college who had been preaching around in the woods of his section of the country. People would say, "Come home with us for dinner." "Come in, Brother-So-and-So, come in!" He came to the college and stayed a few days. Nobody invited him to anything. He just took his place with others there. (That is the way men do in the army when "Uncle Sam" makes soldiers out of them.) After this boy had been at the college a little while he said, "Boys, I am going home; I am somebody at home. People don't even know me around here."

We get a few students here every year who, when they get settled down to the regular grinding routine about this time of the year, begin to show up. You see, they stay here a little while and the light is turned on. They begin to find, and we find, too, that they lack the ability to go through. They can't obey. They can't take it. They haven't the character. They haven't the backbone. And they won't ever be anything. God has fixed it in this world so that only the obedient make good. Remember it takes character to obey. Listen, the shore of time is covered with human wrecks and failures, the people who didn't obey.

The Apostle Paul said, "I put my body under." What for, Paul? "Lest after I have preached to other people, I myself should be a castaway." That was voluntary obedience. He said, "I wrestle with my own body." He threw his body down and stepped on it, and then walked up and said, "Here I am, God. My body cries for things, but I say, 'Shut up, shut up, SHUT UP. Get down there, get down there, get down! Shut up!" He said he beat himself. His old body would get up and he would say, "Get down there. Get down there!" Paul obeyed; what for? To make money? *No!* What for? So he could be a preacher, a missionary to the Gentiles, a man of God to do what God said. Voluntary obedience! God won't let you be disobedient and succeed. As mean and as malicious and as sinful as Hitler is, he lived a restrained life. He obeyed the voice of his convictions.

God won't let you win a prize fight without obedience. Joe Louis obeyed. Joe's stomach said, "I want some biscuits and Alabama syrup." Joe said, "Shut up!" "But Joe, you know on our Alabama farm your old mother and father had sugar cane molasses, and I like it! Joe, my ancestors liked syrup!" Joe said, "Shut up, and quit bothering me!" Joe's stomach said, "Joe, you shouldn't treat me like that; I am hungry!

Joe, how could you be so mean to me? My poor, crying stomach—syrup, Joe, syrup! Hot biscuits, Joe, and butter and syrup—and plenty of it!" Joe said, "Shut up! Shut up. You will ruin me!" And one day under the lights, and with thousands of people there, Joe's hand was held up and somebody said, "The world's champion, Joe Louis!" "Joe, how did you get there?" Joe answers, "I got there by obedience!"

Paul said, "I've fought a good fight." You did what, Paul? "Fought, fought!" You did what? "FOUGHT!" I didn't think you were a fighter. "Oh, don't you believe it. I wrestled not with flesh and blood but with principalities. I have fought a good fight." And you did, Paul. God bless your memory!

He fought a good fight. He finished the course. He didn't go home the second week. He finished the course. He didn't quit when it got hot. *He finished the course!* God Almighty is too big to use quitters.

"I have fought a good fight, I have finished my course, I have kept the faith. I am now ready to be offered, and the time of my departure is at hand." How did you get there, Paul? "I obeyed! I knocked myself down. In the morning I would wake up and say, 'I had a hard day yesterday, a hard day. My, it is comfortable here in bed. I wish I didn't have to get up this morning. But I must preach today!' "

One day people threw rocks at him and left him by the roadside bloody and, they thought, dead. Somebody came along and thought he was dead, and he must have thought so, too. He got so close to heaven that I think he could hear the angels making music on harps of gold. As he pulled himself together I imagine he said, "Oh, it is too bad to come back from heaven like this. I thought I was at home. But I must get up. Let's wash this blood out of my face. I have to preach somewhere today. I must go. I'll be all right in a little while. Don't worry about me."

"To obey is better than sacrifice." You want to be where you can do as you please, some of you, where folks will coddle you, where you won't have to get up in the morning. And you have begun to wonder if you didn't possibly make a little mistake. After all, wasn't it rather nice to do as you pleased? Well, we are running a training camp for God. We are training soldiers of the Cross, men and women to wear the uniform of God and be leaders in a chaotic world. And obedience is the fundamental thing. It is fundamental in all God's program. If you save yourself, you can't save anybody else. Jesus couldn't. You aren't any better than Jesus, are you? He became obedient— obedient unto death! How far have you gone? Death said, "Come here." Jesus looked up to His Father. The Father said, "Go." And Jesus walked down the stairs from the light of heaven to the darkness of earth and for thirty-three years walked toward the cross. Jesus was obedient—obedient unto death.

The whole rotten modern world is wrecked because of disobedience. The sinful, hellish philosophy that has destroyed America is built upon the philosophy of disobedience. Prisons are filled with juvenile delinquents. Children have been killing their school teachers in some sections of America—cutting their throats, shooting them. Little girls and boys are out murdering people. If you stay here you are going to obey.

Dean Edwards, I charge you before God in the presence of these witnesses, do your duty. Rules in this school are made to be kept. Send home the students who won't obey. You owe that to this institution. You owe it to these young people. You owe it to God Almighty on heaven's high throne. You owe it to the cause of the Lord Jesus Christ. We are training leaders here. And obedience is the first essential of leadership. Our Bob Jones College boys in uniform write, "Dr. Bob, thank you." They have written back here and said, "Don't lower your standards." And God helping us, we are not going to do it.

Prayer: "Lord, we are all at the best poor and frail. At our best we are not worth much. We wonder how Thou canst do anything with us. We thank Thee for Jesus Christ Thy Son. He was obedient unto death. If He had been disobedient we never could have been saved. We thank Thee for the obedience of Paul and the obedience of Moses. We thank Thee for the obedience of the servants of God through the ages. And we thank Thee that at Bob Jones College the large percentage of the students like the rules and have voluntarily committed themselves to the program of building Christian character so they can be Christian leaders. Help us in our responsibility! Lord God, don't let the time ever come in this school when we wink at the violation of rules and regulations. Save our country, our lawless America! O Lord God, have mercy upon us. Make us faithful here and keep us true to Thee. For Jesus' sake we ask it. Amen."

The Two Roads

I CALL your attention this morning to the 13th and 14th verses of the 7th chapter of Matthew:

"Enter ye in at the strait gate: for wide is the gate, and broad is the way, that leadeth to destruction, and many there be which go in thereat;

"Because strait is the gate, and narrow is the way, which leadeth unto life, and few there be that find it."

I do not think the Lord is necessarily talking here about the way to heaven and the way to hell. He is talking about the way to life and the way to destruction, not only in this world but in the world to come.

You must remember that the Sermon on the Mount doesn't have much doctrine in it. That is the main reason why modernistic theologians talk much about the Sermon on the Mount and say so little about the *blood* which Jesus shed at Golgotha. The Sermon on the Mount is an enunciation of principles. For instance, Jesus said, "Blessed are the pure in heart; for they shall see God." That has always been so. It is a statement of principle. Jesus didn't tell His audience at this time that He was going to die on a cross and shed His blood so they could have pure hearts and be able to see God.

"Blessed are the peacemakers; for they shall be called the children of God." It doesn't make you a child of God to be a peacemaker, but it is a characteristic of the children of God that they are peacemakers. The characteristic of the devil's crowd is that they are trouble-makers. One of the surest signs that you are God's child is that you have a peaceful, constructive attitude toward life, not destructive. All the destructive elements in human nature are satanic and sinful.

Now, I do not think the Lord is talking here, necessarily, about the life beyond this life. He is talking about the way to successful living and the way to failure, not only in the life to come but also in this life. He says in substance, "There are two gates." I want to tell you about them. One of them is a hard gate. This word "strait" is not spelled "straight" as we spell the word meaning a straight line. It is spelled "s-t-r-a-i-t," meaning *hard*. The other gate is an easy gate. These two gates enter into two roads. One of them is a narrow road; the other is a wide road. On one of these roads, the narrow road, only a few people are traveling. This other road is a popular road. A great many people go that way.

Now, listen, young people, it is hard to get on the road of right. It is always hard. It is never hard to do wrong. It is easy to do wrong. A dead fish can swim downstream. It takes a live fish to swim upstream. The easiest job you ever had on this earth is to do wrong. You don't have to do anything to do wrong except to let go. It is no trouble to sin. It has always been hard to do right. The way of right has never been an easy way. The gate itself is a hard gate. It is hard to start. It is not only hard to start, it is hard to stay put after you start. The road is narrow and you will get off if you don't watch.

I used to think of this narrow road as a road that was walled in like a narrow street in some oriental city. I used to think of it as having a wall on either side so that you had to stay on it. But I don't think that is what is meant.

Did you ever drive a car down a narrow road? I remember years ago I drove an automobile through the mountains in West Virginia. I couldn't find a place to turn around. I had to keep going. I never was up against it in my life as I was then. There was a precipice hundreds of feet deep to my left. I had to keep that narrow road right around the mountain. I couldn't turn around. I dared not move over to one side because there was a precipice over there. Now, that is what I think Jesus is talking about here. This road is a hard road to stay on. It is hard to get started and it is hard to keep going. That has been my experience.

A man said to me some time ago, "The devil never bothers me any more." "Why," I said, "I wouldn't tell anybody that. I would keep that to myself. A man is an awfully sorry fellow when the devil doesn't want him! If he didn't bother me, I wouldn't say anything about it." The devil hounds the path of the man who is going the right way.

Some of you came here this year and found it hard to start. The environment was different from anything you had ever been in in your life. This place wasn't like any place you had ever seen. You weren't used to restrictions. You weren't used to being told what to do. You told your mother what to do. You told your daddy what to do. You told everybody else what to do. Then you came down here and somebody told *you* what to do—like they tell the fellows in the army. You know, you don't talk back to the officer in the army. In this environment it was hard for you to adjust yourself. Some of you thought you never would do it. But you got on the road. You said, "It is difficult." The gate was opened, but it was a hard gate. You got through and you are now on the road. But it is hard to stay on the road. You had better watch your step or you will get off. It is a narrow road.

Listen, young people, I have realized as never before that we are in the minority. That is what Jesus said. He said, "Our crowd is a little crowd." We don't have many people. We never have had many of them. Make up your mind that if you are going this road, the right road, you are not going to be over-crowded. The road is wide enough for everybody who wants to go, but not many folks want to go. It is a narrow road, and people do not like narrow roads. It is a hard gate, and people do not like a hard gate. So, we are in the minority.

That used to hurt me when I was a young fellow. I am naturally a politician. The hardest job I ever had was to stay out of politics. I almost sold out one time to the devil. People wanted me to run for an office, and I came mighty near doing it. It was the greatest temptation I ever had. I like the popular appeal. These politicians deal with the masses. But you don't have any politicians in this country talking about the right. You don't have anybody running for President who stands up and says, "Ladies and gentlemen, this is right." They say, "Ladies and gentlemen, you are not getting a square deal"! They make a selfish appeal. We didn't get prohibition in this country by saying it was right. You couldn't get a prohibition politician to go up and down this country and run a campaign and say, "It is wrong to sell liquor." We used to say that. The old preachers said it. Then later we got to saying, "It is bad for business to sell liquor." And we got the people to give up liquor for a while for business reasons. When you do a thing for business reasons it is a selfish reason. The fellow who does the right thing and does the right thing because it is the right thing to do, regardless of whether it pays him to do the right thing or does not pay him to do the right thing, is the right kind of man.

You couldn't put an issue through in America on the basis that it is right. Listen just a minute! You couldn't have put the United States in war just to protect Greece! I hate to say this. We were sorry for Greece. We were sorry for the Armenian Christians a few years ago. We are sorry for people to be persecuted. But one day we said, "*We* might get persecuted. They might do something to us, too. They are treating the Greeks mean, they are treating a lot of folks mean." So, we started in for self-protection. Even some of the men in Congress stood up and said, "Now, don't fool yourself, we are not philanthropic. We are fighting for ourselves." We have a selfish outlook on life. Most people are like that.

Jesus said, "This is a hard gate and a narrow road, and if you travel it you are going to have to go with a small crowd." If you want to go with a big crowd, check out of Bob Jones College. Make up your mind. When you get back to Boston, or New York, or somewhere down South or out West, you are going to find that you are in the minority. Don't forget that. The

Christian soldier in uniform is with the minority. The boy in the Navy who is walking with God is in the minority. That is what Jesus said. He said, "There are not many going this way. It is a hard way. It is a narrow road, and not many people are traveling it." Jesus said, "The other road is easy to get into—the gate is wide open. And when you get in it, it is a good road, a wonderful road, a broad and well-paved road." There is the surging crowd. There is excitement, and music, and laughter—everybody is having a good time. If you want to know which is the right road, find out the way a few people are going. Find out the way that is hard. If you want to know which is the wrong road, find out the way that is easy. Find out the way that is broad.

I can go into any community in America and tell you which crowd is on the right road and which one is on the wrong road. I can watch the crowds on the streets and the crowds in the churches. The very fact that the road is crowded is proof that it is the wrong road. The wrong road is the popular road. The people on the crowded road crucified Jesus Christ. God's people never have been in the majority and never will be until Jesus Christ comes again.

The first time I ever went to New York City I found myself going down Broadway. All at once I stopped and said, "Where am I going?" Half of the people who go to New York City, or other big cities, just walk. They are not going anywhere. But a fellow is supposed to be going somewhere.

Now, I like a good road. I like a smooth road. I like an easy road, but I don't want the kind of road that will get me to the wrong place. I would rather travel a hard road and come out at the right place.

Let me illustrate. Suppose my mother, who died when I was fourteen years of age, was down in Dalton, Georgia. Suppose in Chattanooga there is music, light, life, laughter, song, happiness; and there is a paved highway to Chattanooga. Suppose there is a muddy, rough, sticky, hard road to Dalton. I can go either way. I can go to either place. I am a free moral agent. I would say, "I am going to Dalton. It is a bad road— I know it. It is a rough road—I know it! I will get stuck in the mud—I know it! But there is somebody down there. Mother is there!" A rough road is not so hard to travel if it leads to some one or something we really love.

Now, Jesus Christ laid down this principle clearly. He said, "This road that is narrow leads to *life*. The broad road leads to destruction." All this wild, sinful crowd, laughing, playing, having a good time and letting go are not on the road that leads to life. They are on the road that leads to destruction. All this carousing crowd, this wild, loud crowd, playing the game loose are on the road that leads to death. Jesus says the popular road, the broad road, the road with an easy, wide-open gate, leads to destruction. The other road leads to life. Listen, young people, if you will go the way you have started, you will go somewhere. You will come out at the end of the road where there is life, where there is contentment, where there is peace, where there is happiness.

I get letters from our Bob Jones College boys in the Army; some of them touch me deeply. Some of them read something like this: "Dear Dr. Bob: You were rather strict when I was there in Bob Jones College.

I used to hear you preach and it seemed to me that some things were rather hard. But how glad I am I went through with it. I have found peace. I have found contentment. I have something the boys around me do not have." You ought to read the letters. They would encourage you to go on down the right road.

Ask the men who have found *life* if they traveled an easy road. I have never had an easy road. It isn't easy to face the world when the world is against you. It isn't easy to stand for something when you have to stand alone. It isn't easy when somebody with a sneer says, "You go to Bob Jones College? Why you are told there when to get up in the morning. There are rules; that college is strict." It isn't easy. Jesus said it wouldn't be easy! Do you know anything around here we stand for that isn't right? If you know something we stand for that isn't right, we will change it. The fellow who wants what he wants whether it is right or wrong is on the road that leads to destruction. The man who wants what is right and has his eye on the goal is willing to walk carefully.

You young people tell the superficial, godless, worldly crowd that we are willing to match the educational standards of Bob Jones College against those of any other institution. Tell them our students come from the best families in practically all the states. Tell them we are not the offscouring of the world. Tell them we have just been scoured off. Tell them we chose to travel the narrow road. Tell them we know where we are going. Tell them we prefer life to destruction and that the road we are traveling leads to life.

You dare not take the easy road. The road of laziness is an easy road. I am lazy and you are lazy. Everybody is lazy. Some of us are not mentally lazy, but we are physically lazy. Some of us are mentally lazy and not physically lazy. I don't believe there is a girl on earth who likes to practice the piano as much as she ought to practice it. Ask the girl who practices the piano if it is easy. It is easy to smoke a cigarette. It is easy to go to a party. Listen! The thing that is damning young people all over America is that they are looking for the easy road. That is what is populating hell.

Let me ask you something: Which road are you on? Now, don't try to fool yourself. I may not be here twenty-five years from now when your hair gets a little gray or a little thin, but I can tell you what you are going to be twenty-five years from now if you will show me whether you are hunting a soft place or a hard place, whether you are looking for a wide road or a narrow road.

There is only one way you can stand this hard gate and this narrow road—just one way—and that is to have a forward look. I have always been the sort of person who wanted to know what was going to happen in the years to come. A man told me who roomed with William Jennings Bryan at College that one day somebody said, "Bill, let's go out and have a good time." Bill said, "Boys, that isn't right. I am going to take care of my body so I can serve my God and my country." You have never heard the name of the boy who said, "Let's go out and have a good time." But who has not heard of William Jennings Bryan? "Strait is the gate, and narrow is the way"; but it leads out at the right place. "Wide is the gate, and broad is the way"; but it leads out at the wrong place. Are you on the right road? If so, stay on it. If you are not on it, get on it now.

Prayer: "Our Father, Jesus talked about a cross. Jesus talked about hardships. Jesus talked about self-crucifixion. Jesus talked about self-sacrifice. Jesus said if we would lose our life we would find it. The devil tells us something else. The devil says, "Take it easy. Do as you please. Live your own life!" Either Jesus is right or the devil is right. Somebody is right and somebody is wrong. We thank Thee, Lord, that even history proves that Jesus is right. Help these young people in Bob Jones College to enter the hard gate and travel the narrow way, unpopular as it is, so some day they may enjoy more abundant life. We ask it in Jesus' name. Amen."

A Divided Kingdom

I WANT to read you the 24th and 25th verses of the 12th chapter of Matthew.

"But when the Pharisees heard it, they said, This fellow [talking about Jesus] doth not cast out devils, but by Beelzebub the prince of the devils. And Jesus knew their thoughts, and said unto them, Every kingdom divided against itself is brought to desolation; and every city or house divided against itself shall not stand."

I call your attention to the last part of the 25th verse: "Every kingdom divided against itself is brought to desolation; and every city or house divided against itself shall not stand."

Jesus said, and remember when Jesus says it, it is so, "Every kingdom divided against itself is brought to desolation; and every city or house divided against itself shall not stand." Jesus didn't mean by that that there wouldn't be a Rome when Rome was divided. He didn't mean there wouldn't be a Greece when division came in Greece. Rome might be Rome and Greece might be Greece; but they wouldn't be the Rome that was and the Greece that was. Division means disintegration.

There is only one way you can gather people and that is to gather people around an idea, a thought, a conviction, a program, or personality. We Christians are supposed to gather around Jesus Christ.

I talked to you yesterday about Bob Jones College —I think I referred to this institution. I usually do when I am speaking anywhere. It doesn't matter where it is, I usually get something in about it. I talked to you yesterday about the two ways, the strait way and the wide way. Jesus says that you can find out which road is the right road. He says that the right road is the road that is hard to get in and hard to stay in. Let me say that again: Jesus says (boiling it down to simple words) that if you want to know what is the right road, find the road that is hard to get in and the road that is hard to stay in, the road that not many people are traveling, and *that* will be the right road. If you want to know the wrong road, find the road that is easy to get in and easy to stay in, the road that is very popular. That will be the wrong road. One road is narrow. The other road is wide. One leads to life. The other is broad and leads to death.

Bob Jones College, I told you, stands for the narrow road. We don't stand for the broad road. We don't stand for what is stood for in most educational institutions. We stand without apology for the old-time Christian philosophy of self-control and self-restraint. This institution is operating in its seventeenth year. All these years we have gathered around an idea: The Bible is the Word of God. Jesus is the Son of God. He died on the cross to save us. We are saved by faith in Him. We stand for "honest-to-goodness" hard work. We stand for honest study. We stand for modesty and virtue for girls and for honesty and uprightness and purity for boys. We stand for the old decencies, the old traditions. The college started off like that. It stands for those things still. We don't apologize to

Mr. Anybody for it. And great prosperity, in spite of bitter opposition, has come to Bob Jones College because of the things for which it stands.

The growth of this institution has been unparalleled in the educational history of America. There is only one other evangelistic, orthodox college in America that has enrolled more students than we have this year. The other college to which I refer, and it is a good college, is nearly ninety years old. Our institution has more students than the other college had at the end of seventy-five years. As far as I can find, there has never been anything in the history of America like the record Bob Jones College has made. In all the educational history of this nation, this thing is unparalleled.

Here we are today in the midst of war with a thirty per cent increased enrollment over last year and with nobody in uniform, all civilian students. We have a reasonable number of men students, and we have sent our share of men into the armed service. There is a large increase in the enrollment of women students. We have the largest freshman class we have ever had in the history of the college. I opened my mail today and there were applications for the second semester. There were not fewer than ten requests for catalogs, and several wrote asking if we could take them the second semester. This movement is evidently of God.

We have never been a divided college. The minute this school becomes divided, Jesus said, it will not stand. He didn't mean there wouldn't be a Bob Jones College. He meant it would not be the Bob Jones College that God meant it to be. We move here in mass. That doesn't mean that we agree about every policy or method or program. It doesn't mean that we are a bunch of nonentities. But we are all rallying around a truth, a purpose, a program.

We never have a division in our faculty. Let me tell you young people something. The faculties of many colleges I know in America are divided. In most universities and colleges teachers knife one another; they backbite, they criticize one another. They are jealous of one another. Sometimes they despise one another.

We are in an awful mess in America. Go to the average school or university today and you will find strife between fraternity men and non-fraternity men, sorority women and non-sorority women. You are in a school where we don't have anything like that. If you are good enough to be in this college, you are good enough to be in anything in the college. We have no select groups here that get in the fraternities and sororities and separate themselves from everybody else. We are of one mind in this school. We have not always had smooth sailing, but we have thrown the Jonahs overboard. If we get a Jonah on the ship, and the ship doesn't take him, we let the fish eat him! We throw him overboard.

When I started a college I had enough experience to know that the thing to do was to gather people of like mind around an idea, gather them around a program, gather them around a standard. If people unite on that, all hell can't shake them. Such people can shake their fists in the face of the devil and tell him to "go to."

"United we stand, divided we fall." That is the reason that in this school we have no "griping." Gripers are not welcome here. If you are a dirty griper you are not one of us. You don't have to gripe here. You can walk into the president's office, the acting president's office, the dean's office, the business manager's office and say, "I'd like to ask you about something." The youngest student in this school will get the same hearing as the president of the student body. The rights and the liberties of the humblest student in this school will be protected.

I don't know how long I am going to be here. I don't know how long I am going to live. I don't know how long Bob, Jr., will be here. I am not speaking for Bob now; I am speaking for the old man. The old man is talking to you. As long as the old man is here we are going to have a kingdom that isn't divided. And every student in this school has an obligation to God Almighty and to future generations to preserve the united, sweet, beautiful spirit here. The very minute you pull down the flag of this school one inch, *one inch!* or break into the harmony or purpose of the program, or put one unnecessary burden on it, you are an enemy to the things for which this college stands. You are sinning against God, for this school stands for God and His cause.

Several years ago I spoke to Grace Livingston Hill about a certain college. I could call the name of the college and you would know it. It is one of the most modernistic colleges in America, a college that stands for the behavioristic, satanic philosophy of life—the philosophy of "do as you please, go to class when you want to go; if you don't want to go, don't go." Grace Livingston Hill said, "Dr. Jones, I used to do personal work in that school. In the old days the school had revivals and a mourners' bench. I used to go down the aisle, bring a girl up to the front, get her on her knees, and get her converted." That school, which started off as a spiritual, conservative Christian college stands today in America for everything contrary, in a spiritual sense, to the purpose of the founders of the institution. And listen! American is filled with universities and colleges like it!

Recently I was in a certain city—I won't name it. You can guess it, but you can't say I told you! It was a city in New England. I was talking to a spiritual, conservative, evangelical minister of the Gospel. I said, "Where did you get your theology?" He said he got it in a certain near-by university, naming the university. It is a denominational institution. It was founded by orthodox Christians—Christians who believed the Bible from cover to cover. "Well," I said, "what kind of place is it?" "Oh," he said. "you know _____" (naming another university, a great modernistic university which everybody knows about). The same person runs both universities." "Oh," I said, "sure enough! I didn't know there was any connection between them." "Yes," he said, "the same person runs both of them." I asked, "Who is it?" He said, "The devil. In one of them he has agents to stand up and talk in pious tones. Sometimes they even use orthodox language. The other one is openly modernistic. But if I had to choose between the two, I would prefer the one which doesn't call itself Christian." Remember that university had a Christian beginning.

We have all hell to contend with, but, God helping, us, we are going to keep Bob Jones College a kingdom that isn't divided and a house that stands together.

When I was a young preacher I used to try to sell

programs to people. I would set up a program and go
out and say, "I want to sell you this program." I would
try to sell the program. When I got along in years
I learned that wasn't right. I don't try to sell programs
any more. I set up programs. Everybody that has an
affinity for the program will come to it. If you are
drawn to a program because you have an affinity for
the program, it will be worth something to you and
you will be worth something to the program. It wears
you out to keep selling the same thing to the same
people every day, and then you can't always keep
them sold. But you don't have to sell the fellow whose
heart has an affinity for the program. The Bible says,
"They that know God hear us." We don't make them
hear us. We say, "The Lord Jesus Christ died to save
sinners." A fellow hears us and says, "Listen. Did
you hear that? Let's go over with them." The young
man or the young woman who has an affinity for
spirituality, upon learning the things for which we
stand, just gravitates to the college.

Somebody says, "You know, I would like to have
Bob Jones in my church but he would get some money
for Bob Jones College." Why, we have no financial
schemes. Most of the schools have agents all around
the country raising money. We don't do that.

There is something else we don't do, too. We don't
have people out over the whole country getting students.
Most of these schools have all the preachers and laymen
lined up to get students. We don't do that. We just
tell everybody in America, "Bob Jones College believes
the Bible from cover to cover. Bob Jones College believes in the old-time religion. Bob Jones College believes in decency. Bob Jones College believes in honest,

thorough work. Bob Jones College believes in high educational standards." We say to mothers, "Mothers have sent their daughters to Bob Jones College and never has one gone back home in disgrace and shame." We just tell the folks about it. People say, "That sounds good to me. That is what I am looking for." "They that know God hear us." We gather around a standard. That is the way Bob Jones College operates. That is the reason you are here. Your mother wanted you at this place. That friend told you about it; or you yourself wanted to come. I thank God for the decent young people who want to come.

Once in a while I want to sit down and review this thing. We stand for God. We stand for honest work. We don't stand for lazy loafers. We don't stand for girls who won't study and boys who won't work. We don't ask you to pass an examination. We ask you to do your best to pass it. It is no disgrace to fail on an examination in this school. It is a disgrace to do less than your best to keep from failing. Just do your best—that is all we ask you to do. Do your "dead-level" best, shoot straight, be honest, be upright, stand for the things the school stands for.

I can take this crowd here, faculty members and you young people, and we can lick hell. Why, listen! There is an army here this morning! And the banner over us is the flag of the Cross. Forward march! Don't kick a fellow-soldier. If you don't like the way the flag is carried, grow up and maybe you can carry it some day. Maybe the fellow who is carrying it is carrying it the best he can. Listen, you have good teachers, loyal teachers, Christian teachers—teachers who pray for you, teachers who love you, teachers who are interested in you. There

isn't a question in the minds of the administration
about the loyalty and co-operation of a single member
of our faculty. There has never been such union and
brotherhood and sweetness. It wasn't in the school I
attended. It isn't in any church where I preach. The
churches are not like it. Many of them are split and
divided. A house divided against itself may be a house,
but it will not be the home that God meant it to be.
I want Bob Jones College always to be what God meant
it to be.

Prayer: "O Lord God, help us to be faithful and
true here, true to the principles, true to the creed, true
to the standards, true to the spirit. Help us to know
there is more than a creed. There is a spirit. Help us
to live true to the spirit! And keep this thing going!
Keep us all marching on! Bless us that we may know
what to do in the future.

"Lord, we want to do what Thou dost want us to
do. We are so blind and so frail. Lead us by Thy Spirit
and give us wisdom from above, not the wisdom from
beneath. This wisdom down here is worthless. Give
us the wisdom that comes down from Heaven. And,
Lord, bless these boys and girls. We thank Thee for the
prayer groups and prayer captains. We thank Thee for a
faculty about which we do not have to worry. O Lord
God, keep us true! Keep this school true! Thou hast
been so good to us that it almost frightens us. Keep
us faithful! We pray in Jesus' name. Amen."

Too Lazy to Plow

I HAVE a verse of Scripture about which I want to talk to you. I want to drive it home to your hearts. I pray God to bless us as we try to think about it together. It is the 4th verse of the 20th chapter of Proverbs.

"The sluggard will not plow by reason of the cold; therefore shall he beg in harvest, and have nothing."

That is what God's Word says. You talk about good, common sense! You won't get in all other literature as much common sense as you get out of the Bible. If you want to know how to succeed, learn how from the Bible. If you want to know about salesmanship, study the Bible. You can get out of the Bible more good, practical, common sense than you can get in all the other literature in the world.

Now, get this text this morning. If you turn back from difficulty you will go hungry some day, or somebody else will have to feed you. All the failures I've ever met in my life were people who turned back when they met difficulties. Here is a student who comes to Bob Jones College and gets up against it. Then he begins to try to find an excuse to back off, an excuse to get home, an excuse to go back to mama. Occasionally a student will build up the most pious reasons. "The Lord has led me to go back to take care of my mother. I shouldn't stay here, I should go back and be kind to my daddy, my poor old daddy! He needs me so bad!" The only thing wrong with that student is that he is too rotten lazy to study. You know there is nothing in the world that makes me so disgusted as to have a fellow offer a pious excuse for doing something that is not pious. I get *so* tired of the shams and humbugs I meet along life's way.

The worth-while things in life are difficult. You show me the kind of difficulty you can drive through, and I'll tell you what you are, what kind of character you have. We read here in the Bible in one of these Proverbs that a fellow wakes up in the morning and says, "There is a lion in the street." He won't get up. He is a sluggard. The very thing that should make him get up, keeps him in bed. If there is a lion in the street he ought to get up. He ought to do something about it. But he wakes up and sits up in bed. There he is with the cover tucked about him. He says, "There is a lion in the street! There's a lion in the street! There is a lion in the street." And he lies back down. He lets the lion eat up somebody. Say, if there is a lion in the street, *get up!* That is the very time you ought to get up. *Do* something!

The sluggard wakes up and says, "Well, it is too cold to plow today. I don't like this kind of weather. I will just stay in bed." All right, buddy, wait until harvest time when folks around you have a good crop. *You* will be starving, and the fellow who plowed in the cold will have something to eat.

Do you know that a big percentage of the human race are dependents? And the reason usually is, they didn't plow when it was cold. They turned back from the difficulties of life. You are going to meet difficulties. Listen! The greater God's purpose in your life, the greater will be the difficulties you will have to face. If you study the records of the men who have moved the world for God, you will find they were always men who drove through great difficulties. There is no royal, easy road to success.

I never shall forget the time I heard Paderewski play. Somebody said I couldn't enjoy classical music. I didn't know anything about classical music. The reason people don't enjoy classical music is that they just don't get much of it. Even ordinary people like the classical when they get it. Some things are palmed off for the classical when they are not classical. But I went to hear him play, expecting to be bored to death. I sat back there just a poor, old, blundering country man without any knowledge of music; but my soul was thrilled. I never shall forget how as I watched him play my heart was moved. Somebody said to me, "Did you know he travels on the train with his piano in his special car and spends hours and hours a day practicing?" Just think of it! Some people don't make musicians because they are too lazy to practice. They have musical hearts but lazy fingers!

You know, downright laziness is what is the matter with most people. Just too good-for-nothing, no-account, lazy—that is all. Somebody has to feed them, has to bring them something to eat. Now, this is what God says about it. I am just telling you in modern words what God says in classical language. God says the sluggard who won't plow when it is cold, begs when harvest comes. That is what God's Word says about it. Now you are going to have to learn to plow when it is cold. Don't be looking out for your comfort. Don't be looking for a nice place to sit down.

Sometimes a student comes here all pepped up. He is going to do big things. He uses Christian language —talks pious. But once you put him to work, his spiritual barometer drops. You say, "Now, buddy, you are going to get down and work today. Hit the routine!" He won't be shouting when he gets his nose in a mathematics book. Personally, I never could shout over a problem in geometry! When you get to digging into Greek you won't be "Amen-ing" much. But there is as much religion in working a problem in mathematics as there is in saying "Hallelujah" at a camp meeting. And I haven't any respect for a young man who says "Hallelujah" at a camp meeting who won't dig out his lessons in an honest, faithful way when he is in college.

You are in one place that believes in "the old-time religion" and good, everyday common sense. "Amens" don't take the place of sweat in this school. Buddy, you will mop your brow many a time this year. You won't know it is cold! If you don't like to work, you are in the wrong pew. Listen, listen! We won't see you for dust, you will be moving around here so fast. You will be running around and you will be so tired your tongue will be dragging almost between your legs when you go across the campus. I am telling you about it, and I am not overestimating it. This is going to be the "out-workingest" working year you ever worked in your life! We have made up our minds to it.

Always before this year we opened school on a Wednesday morning. We opened on Tuesday night this year. We never got down to real business in past years until about Monday. This is what—Friday? This is Friday, and we are running on full schedule. And we are going to do next Tuesday's work tomorrow. That is going some! We are getting down to business! And we don't want you begging us for some of our wheat when harvest comes. If you are not going to work, don't hang around here. Don't you be a lazy loafer around here and then when we get a good crop come up and say, "I'd like to have a biscuit." We want to eat our own "grub." If you are too lazy to plow when it is cold, then just starve. You know St. Paul said, "If they won't work, don't let them eat." Mel Trotter said, "I have seen many a religious 'bum,' but I never saw a Christian tramp in my life." Listen, I never knew God to let any man down who worked and prayed and trusted. The college word this year is *"Pray!"* Pray! Pray! Pray! PRAY! But we haven't taken that word *"Work"* out of our vocabulary.

"Work wins." God won't do for you what you can do for yourself. I have told these old students—and now you new ones listen: God Almighty is not going to master mathematics for you. One day a student came to me and said, "I've been praying the Lord to help me pass my examinations." "Well," I said, "He's not going to do a thing for you. Do you suppose God Almighty is going to endorse your laziness?" Think about a fellow who doesn't study coming to God and saying, "Now, Lord, I was too rotten lazy to study and I want You to help me out." God would say, "I won't help you. I don't endorse your laziness." God won't do for you what you can do for yourself.

You go out and start to walk across the street out there. You say, "I'm going to trust the Lord. I am going to shut my eyes and walk across the street. Now, Lord, take care of me; I am trusting You." You try that, and some fool will run over you. You will get hit on both sides! If you get out there and start walking across the street, the thing to do is to use both eyes and pray, too. Even then some fool may run over you.

Amanda Smith, that great colored woman whom God raised up and used in such a wonderful way—just a poor washerwoman, a maid—one time found that she couldn't hear in one of her ears. She got anointed and asked the Lord to heal her. She just kept on asking the Lord to heal her. But she got worse and worse. One day Amanda went to see the doctor. She said, "Doctor, I asked the Lord and He didn't do anything for me; see what you can do." She had good sense. She had asked the Lord, but she went around to see a doctor and said, "Look in that ear, Doctor, and see what is in it." The doctor just got a little wax out and she could hear. Old Amanda said, "The trouble was I wanted the Lord to wash my ears for me!" There are some people who want the Lord to wait on them. God is not going to clean your ears for you. Wash your own dirty ears! Don't you ask God to press your pants. He is not your tailor! If you are too lazy to press your pants or get them pressed, He will let them bag off you!

There was a woman one time who had a boy in our school. He was in high school. (Warning bell rings) Just a minute—I want to finish with this boy. That woman sent that boy here to our Academy. He was a little "ornery" fellow. The mother wrote me a letter and said she was praying he would come out all right. I said, "Your boy doesn't need prayer. He needs an energetic mother with a stick." God won't whip a mother's "kid" for her. He will let her heart break sometimes because she didn't whip him! The God I worship has good sense. The God I serve is a God who is infinite in wisdom. God sends the sunshine, God sends the rain. God gives the soil. God gives you the physical strength to plow; and if you are too lazy to plow, God won't send you any wheat when harvest comes.

Now, let's get down to business. You know, all of us are lazy. I've always been lazy. If I am lazy, what about *you?* Nobody ever accused me of being lazy, but I am. I have been accused of everything in the world but being lazy and running. I never ran away from a fight and never was accused of being lazy. But I'm lazy. Everybody is lazy. I don't like to study except what I like to study. I don't like to work. I sweated here this summer in my office, when I would have given almost anything in the world to have had a vacation.

If you start off in life backing off from everything except just what you want to do and leaving undone what you don't want to do, you will never amount to a "hill of beans." God won't let you make good. Some young people go off to school and take just what they want to take, just what they like. That is what is the matter with the world now. Everybody in this school ought to take some subject he hates. Every student ought to have to do something he despises to do, and then do it well. If you haven't taken some subject this year that you don't like, there is something wrong with your character. Under the old educational system we were told what to take. We were told that what we disliked most, we needed most. That old system worked, too.

Now, what did God say, What did God say makes men beg? He said men beg because they will not go out in the cold. They will not plow unless the weather suits them!

Prayer: "Our Father, save us from being lazy. Save us from mental laziness. Save us from physical laziness. Save us from spiritual laziness. Some of us are too lazy to pray. Help us to learn to plow when it is cold. Help us not to turn back when the sun gets hot. Help us to not turn away from mathematics, or science, or literature, or history, or whatever we ought to take. Help us to do what God wants us to do. And may we go through with Thee this year to victory so after a while when harvest time comes we can gather in the sheaves for the glory of God. We ask it in Thy name! Amen."

Bearing the Yoke

"It is good for a man that he bear the yoke in his youth."

THIS text is found in Lamentations 3: 27. In order to understand it, let us get clearly fixed in our minds the intention and purpose of a yoke. When I was a boy I thought that when Jesus said, "Come unto Me, all ye that labor and are heavy laden . . . Take My yoke upon you, and learn of Me," He wanted to put a burden on me. That isn't so at all. When Jesus wants to put a yoke on a man, He wants to hitch that man up to the burden not to make it heavy for him, but to make it so he can carry the burden. A yoke is not intended to burden the ox but to make it possible for the ox to pull the load. The burden must be carried. The wagon must be pulled. And the yoke is put on the ox so he can pull the load.

You are going through life with burdens upon you. You can't escape. There is no way out. Even if you don't have anything to do, you will have the burden of time on your hands. Somebody told me about a great educator who when he was dying said, "O God, give me life beyond this life and give me something to do." The most miserable people on earth, the heaviest burdened people I have ever seen, have been people with nothing to do—people with the burden of nothing upon them. If you don't have anything to do, you will have time dragging heavily on your hands. You will be running around with no purpose in life, burdened with the passing of the day. You can't escape a burden.

The Bible says that it is a good thing to yoke a fellow up while he is young. I don't take any stock in the modern idea in this country that children shouldn't be made to work. We have, of course, put children in factories when they shouldn't have been put in factories. We have put them to work under dirty conditions. That is bad. But I believe many of the young people of today would have been better off working under dirty conditions than to have been shielded and protected as they have been from all kinds of work and responsibilities. I don't believe in putting little children in dirty places to work—places where they are exposed to disease germs and all that sort of thing. But I would rather see them grow up like that than to see them grow up as many of them grow up today with no responsibility, no burden, carried around in mother's arms, with daddy holding an umbrella over the little darlings so no sun heat can ever hit them.

I don't like hothouse plants. I like flowers that bloom out in the woods and look up into the sky and defy the winds! I don't care for these little plants that have to be carried in at night!—"Send the little darling home; she hurt her toe." "My precious little child sneezed, I am uneasy about her!" When I was a boy down in southeast Alabama the unfit died. Only the fit survived!

I used to get up in the morning and walk three miles to school. I would take my little tin bucket—did you ever take food to school in a tin bucket? We would put the biscuits in while they were hot—we had *hot* biscuits in those days—and put the ham in while it was hot—we used to have ham in that country! Ham or eggs, and plenty of it, was the regular morning diet. The hot ham and hot biscuits would be put into the tin bucket. We didn't need any water in the middle of the day. We just drank that which was left from the steam inside the bucket when the lid was taken off! We would take our little tin buckets and go down the road to school. The rain didn't stop us. The cold didn't stop us. We trudged our way for three miles there and three miles back.

We walked into the schoolroom and sat down. The benches we sat on didn't have backs to them. Backs to benches in those days would have been in the way. The teacher couldn't have got to the students when he used the switch. Little country boys would come in with one little home-made "gallus" fastened on one side in front with a nail and on the other side in the back with a splinter. We called them "one-gallus boys." They looked pale and bad, some of them, and later, scientists said they had hook worms; but the worms didn't hook them! They went on in spite of the hook-worms!

When I was a boy, boys were reared to be men. They were put to plowing and hoeing and working. In those days parents believed that the Bible was right when it said that it is a good thing to yoke up children when they are young, for they will be men and women some day. In the schoolroom we would say to the teacher, "Will you work this problem for me?" She would say, "Work it yourself! That is what you are here for." We would go back and work and come back up and say, "I can't get the answer." She would say, "Go back there and work that problem out!" Now the teachers work them for children.

The old country mothers used to chew for their babies. You laugh at that, but your mama may have chewed for you in another way. She may never have taught you to use your jaws very much, figuratively speaking. She may have picked up after you. Some young people drop everything they have—they don't have much to drop, but they drop everything they do have wherever they are. Mother comes along and picks it up. She picks up dirty shoes and puts them out of the way. Not many children in our day are taught to do anything. They don't know what it means to be hitched up when they are young to the responsibility of hanging up their own clothes. God says that it is bad for children to be reared like that.

Listen! if you don't learn while you are young to take the yoke of responsibility you will never amount to anything! My Bible says something about the man who is faithful in little things being given big things to do when he is needed for the big things. If you are the president of your society and you neglect your responsibility, then if you ever get to be a governor you won't make a good governor. If you are going to lead the prayer meeting and you don't prepare to lead it and don't do your "dead level best" when you get there, God Almighty will never trust you with a big job when you get out in the world.

God leans over the battlements of Heaven today and looks down on Bob Jones College. I think He calls the angels and says, "Do you see that boy yonder? You can depend on him. His business is to pick up

papers on the campus and he picks them up! See that
boy yonder who works in the kitchen? He saw that
the toast was hot. See that fellow yonder? He dusts
the furniture; he is one of the cleaning boys Mr.
Johnson (the business manager) asks to meet four or
five times a day." God says, "Do you see that young
teacher yonder in Bob Jones College, teaching this
year for the first time? She is in her room tonight
getting ready to teach tomorrow. She sees her responsibility. She has an obligation to God and she will
discharge it, God helping her."

Get under the yoke while you are young. God is
going through the earth today looking for people. There
are not many real folks left. There is not much backbone in this country. There is not much character in
this country. We have kept people alive by modern
science and we have reared a generation of great big,
overgrown babies. You don't have to make any effort
to live today. The doctor will give you sulfa drugs to
keep you from dying with pneumonia. Sulfa drugs
work for you. In the old days we had to build a body
that would keep pneumonia from killing us.

Did you ever sit down and ask yourself this question:

"If everybody in Bob Jones College were just like me,
    What kind of a college would my college be?"

Did you ever ask yourself the question:

"If every Christian in this country were just like me,
    What kind of a country would my country be?"

Some of you stop when you meet difficulties. Suppose
your forefathers had done that when they put foot

on American soil? Those old Puritans came over here because they wanted religious liberty. Think what it would mean to go into a wilderness to build a civilization where Indians had to be killed off, where trees had to be cut down! Those folks didn't write over to America to say, "I should like to have a room with a private bath!" They had women in those days, too—not only men, but women, too! When a man married one of those women he was getting a wife. You could eat *her* biscuits and you didn't have to go around all the time protecting her.

My good old country mother had twelve children. I am the eleventh. If they had stopped at ten there wouldn't have been any preacher in the family. I am glad I got here! My mother could take care of a half dozen babies and not have enough to do to keep her busy! Now it takes the husband, the wife, the nurse, and the whole neighborhood to take care of one little brat!

When this war is over, when the boys come back home, when jobs are started, and the wheels of commerce begin to move along the lines of peace, we are going to be looking for folks in this country. They won't ask what school you attended or where you were graduated. They are going to ask if you have the stuff in you. Somebody said to me not long ago, "They laid off a good many people so they let me go." Let me tell you about these folks who lay people off. They always start with the one who is the poorest person in the organization. Then they go on up the line. If I wanted to fire somebody in Bob Jones College to cut down the operating overhead, where would I start? I would say, "Who is the least useful around here?" I would sit down and think it over and I would get rid of them in the order of the one who was the least useful. There never has been a time, and there never will come a time in this world, when you will be out of work if you are really efficient. If you are efficient and there is no place for you in somebody else's business, you will create your own business.

Let me talk about myself a little. I am interested in myself, and I never was very modest about talking about myself. Suppose nobody would let me preach. Suppose the Baptists and Methodists and Presbyterians and the other denominations should shut all the doors of all the churches in America to me. Do you suppose I would quit preaching? I would like to see any ecclesiastical machine stop me from preaching! I would rent me a vacant store and hang out a shingle. I would try to get the people to come in. If they didn't come in I would get out on the street where they were. You can't be stopped if you learn how when you are young to wear the yoke. I got hitched up when I was a boy. I plowed when I was nine years old. Somebody says, "Poor little fellow!" Don't "Poor little fellow me"! Sympathize with the lazy loafers who didn't plow.

My old country daddy wasn't a scholar but he was good with a switch and he had character. When I was ten and eleven years old he would put me on a wagon loaded with vegetables and start me off to town before day. I was always afraid of the dark. I would see the pine trees dancing out by the side of the road, but I had to be in town by daylight, for people got up in those days when I was a boy. You think you get up early here, but when I was a boy we had done half a day's work by the time most of you get up. I drove around in that town, rang door bells, and sold vegetables. I would take an armful of turnips, greens, collards, cabbage, field peas (I am getting hungry!), butter and eggs and milk and sell them. I would take in all the money I could and then drive home about the middle of the day.

One day my father said that if I would get a certain amount of money and would bring it to him I could have anything that was left over. Well, I gave the customers good measure that day, but I didn't heap up the measure. I was honest all right, but I didn't give them anything they weren't entitled to! I made one quarter for myself. I know that amount of money doesn't look like anything to you, but that was money when I was a boy. You could almost rear a family on that amount! There has been more money already spent on little Jimmy, Jr., (young son of the Dean of the college) than it took to bring up a "kid" in my country! On my way home I took that quarter out and looked at it. I had earned it by the little exercise of raking the top off the measuring vessel. But I dropped it. It fell through the wagon into the sand. I stayed there until sundown sifting sand but never did find it! I drive over that road sometimes now with a pain in my heart. I learned that day a lesson. Things don't always turn out as you think they will turn out.

I learned many other lessons, too. I learned that loved ones would die. I learned that poverty would come. I learned that you would figure a thing one way and it would turn out some other way. I learned those lessons when I was young. You had better learn them while you are young. And you had better learn to wear the yoke while you are learning.

I know what you are going to be some day. You are going to be what you are now. If you are a shirker now, you will be a shirker in life. If you are thorough now, you will be thorough in the years ahead of you. If you are a dirty flirt, worming your way into the heart of a boy or girl by subtle, feigned, lying methods, you will be a dirty flirt in the world. Listen! They always run true to form, always! If you are not dependable now, you won't be dependable ten years from now. If you aren't loyal to Bob Jones College, you probably won't be loyal to your wife when you get one. If you are not loyal, you just aren't made up right!

Young people, when I get back here next Tuesday we shall be in the year 1944. I want you to make up your minds as you close this year and go into the next year to put the yoke on. Any job you have ahead of you, do it. Do it right! If you are not going to do it, don't take the job. Listen, if you are going to be on vespers, do your "dead level best"! If you are to push a button around here, push it right! If you turn on these lights, turn them on right! If you are a stage hand, be the right kind of stage hand. If it is your business to pull the curtain down, pull it down on time and do it right! If you have lessons to get, get them! If you have work to do, do that work and do it right!

I used to break yearlings. Some of you don't know what a yearling is. It is a young ox. I used to break them. I didn't expect a yearling to pull what an ox could pull. We had a wagon which suited the yearling's capacity and a wagon which suited the capacity of the ox, but we expected the yearling to pull up to the limit of his ability. We don't expect you to be a middle-aged man at the age of twenty or a middle-aged woman at

the age of twenty. We don't expect you to pull the
load that some of us can pull who have been hitched
up to the harness for so many years. But we expect
you, every one of you in Bob Jones College, to pull to
the limit of your capacity at your age. "It is good for
a man that he bear the yoke in his youth."

Prayer: "Our Father, help these young people. We
thank Thee for the sincerity of the hearts of these
students. We thank Thee for their desires and purposes
and ambitions. We thank Thee for what we have been
able by the grace of God to achieve in this school in
such a short time. We have had a hard time keeping
up the standards for ourselves and for the organization.
It would have been easy so many times to have let go.
And we have been so tempted to do it. But we have
remembered that we had a responsibility here and we
have tried to be faithful in wearing the yoke. It has
been a little heavy sometimes. We felt mighty good
when we could even take it off to get a little sleep at
night. But we thank Thee after all that Thy yoke is
easy and Thy burden is light. Help everybody in this
auditorium this morning to get under the yoke with
the Lord Jesus Christ. If He pulls on one side and we
pull on the other, He will never let it get too heavy
for us. Help us to be faithful and true to Him, and
may the coming year, 1944, be the most marvelous,
the most wonderful, the most victorious year that any
one of us has ever had. May the coming semester be
a blessed time for all of us! Bless the students who
are going to be with us. Bless those who have wavered
between going and staying. Bless those new students
who are coming in. Help us to find a place for them
to sleep and a way to take care of them. Help us to be

prepared to take care of them spiritually. Help us all today to rededicate ourselves to the task and the responsibility. May the vesper programs the second semester be the most wonderful in the history of the school. May everybody be efficient up to the limit of his capacity and ability. May the Bible conference be a time of such blessing as we have never known, and may we close out here at Commencement with a mighty wave of power and glory and blessing sweeping over this place. Thou hast been mighty good to us this year. We haven't had any serious illness. Thou hast watched over us and protected us and helped us. We thank Thee! Now, we want to go along with Thee. Our hearts would say this morning:

"Have Thine own way, Lord! Have Thine own way!
　Thou art the Potter; we are the clay.
Mold us and make us after Thy will,
　While we are waiting, yielded and still."

Mold us and make us according to Thy plan, and do in us and with us and through us and to us whatever Thy will is for our lives. We ask this in the name of Jesus Christ our Lord. Amen."

"Rabbit - Chasers"

I AM bringing you this morning a message on the subject of "Rabbit-Chasers." The subject may sound somewhat out of place for a chapel address in a Christian college. You will, however, keep in mind that the God who made birds also made rabbits. Jesus talked about birds. He said that His Father who, by the way, is our Father too if we are Christians, marked the sparrow's fall. Jesus also talked about dogs. He called one of the rulers of His day an old fox. So, it is all right if I want to talk about rabbits.

When I was a boy in southeast Alabama we used to have great fun at this season of the year hunting opossums. We did not say "O-possums". We said "possums." All hunters wanted good "possum dogs." Many of the best possum dogs in the country were plain, ordinary, cur dogs. We did not judge them by their ancestors. Most of the dogs had no certificates of birth and they had no family trees. One of the best possum dogs I ever saw was an old, mangy, cur dog that nobody would have wanted for any other purpose except to hunt possums.

There was a type dog that nobody wanted. It was a rabbit-chasing dog. Sometimes that type dog would go down a possum trail until he reached a point where a rabbit trail had crossed the possum trail, then he would leave the possum trail and follow the rabbit

trail. Everybody in our section of the country had
contempt for that kind of dog. We all liked good
rabbit dogs. We liked to chase rabbits and we did this
often, but when we had a dog on a possum trail we
expected him to stay on the trail until he got the possum up a tree. About the worst thing anybody could
say about a dog in our country when I was a boy was
to call him a rabbit-chaser.

Most people are rabbit-chasers. Some of you students
are rabbit-chasers. You came to college with your
mind made up to finish your education and equip
yourself for Christian leadership. You stayed on this
possum trail of your purpose until one day you came
to a point where the rabbit of love had crossed the
possum trail of your purpose. You took a whiff, left the
possum trail, and took off after the rabbit of love. Now,
it is all right to chase a rabbit of love; but it is never
right to leave the possum trail of God's purpose for
your life and chase a rabbit of love. When you get
the possum up a tree or, in other words, when you
complete the purpose that God had for you, then it is
all right to go back and chase a rabbit. It is never
right to leave the possum trail of God's plan for your
life and go after any rabbit of any kind that crosses
the trail.

It may be that one of you listening to me now came
to Bob Jones College feeling that God had called you
to a definite field of service. You had sense enough to
know that a call to serve carries with it a call to prepare
to serve. Your mind was made up when you came
here to stay on the possum trail until you treed the
possum, until you completed your training. One day
the rabbit job crossed your path. You got a whiff of

the rabbit trail and left the possum trail of preparation. You went off after the rabbit job. The probabilities are that when you catch the rabbit it will not be worth having, and it is absolutely certain that rabbit-chasers never tree possums.

All of you Bob Jones College students claim to be Christians. All of you say that you have trusted Jesus Christ as your personal Saviour. Some of you came here unsaved, but you have found God since you came. You pray day by day, "Thy kingdom come. Thy will be done in earth, as it is heaven." Do you mean it when you pray for God's will to be done? Or are you just saying it with your lips? God has a will for your life. Some of you are on the possum trail of the Divine purpose. It is up to you to decide whether you are going to stay on the possum trail or whether you are going to be a rabbit-chaser as long as you live. A large percentage of professing Christians are rabbit-chasers. They are on the possum trail today. They will chase rabbits tomorrow. What are you going to be, a possum dog or an "ornery," good-for-nothing rabbit-chaser?

If you will study the lives of the people who have succeeded in this world you will find they were people who stayed on the trail. "This one thing I do," says the Apostle Paul, "I haven't time for anything else. I am called to be an apostle. I am separated unto the job. I am on the trail; and it doesn't matter what happens, I am going to stay on the trail. You can't knock me off the trail! You can't beat me off the trail! You can't call me off the trail." Figuratively speaking, Paul got the possum up the tree. He stayed on the trail of God's purpose for his life. One day he got to be an old man. He sat down and wrote a young man and said, "I have kept the faith. I have finished the course."

The Apostle Paul chased the possum of God's purpose for his life across the Mediterranean. He chased it into the palace of kings. He ran it through the courthouse. The judge himself couldn't call him off the trail! He was beaten and was left by the roadside, bloody. He got up and took another "whiff," and kept running. He chased that possum through dismal dungeons. But he stayed on the trail! God never used any man who left the possum trail to chase rabbits.

God has a will for your life. God has a purpose back of your existence. God has revealed His will and His purpose to some of you. Some of you got on the trail, but you didn't stay there. You got a whiff of a rabbit and said, "Well, I think a rabbit will satisfy me. I would rather catch a rabbit tonight than run a possum through the woods and across the creek and up the hill and then up a tree. A rabbit is all right. A rabbit is just as good as a possum anyway."

A rabbit is all right, if God made you to be a rabbit-chaser. If God meant for you to be a stenographer, then being a stenographer is just as divine a job as being a queen. If God meant for you to plow in the field, then plowing in the field is just as sacred as standing in a pulpit. If God Almighty meant for you to be a carpenter, then being a carpenter is as holy a job for you as wearing a priestly robe or singing in the choir. But if God put you on a possum trail, it is a sin to chase rabbits! You have no right to do it! Stay on the trail! Don't turn back. Go through with it! The men who have gone places for God have always been the men who stayed on the possum trail.

The Son of God came all the way from heaven to this earth. I am speaking reverently. He got on the trail of His Father's will. Everything tried to stop Him, but He stayed on the trail. One day as He had a little group about Him He said, "I must go to Jerusalem." One of His disciples said, "Don't go—far be it from You!" Jesus said, "Get behind me, Satan." "Where are You going?" we ask Jesus. "I am going to Jerusalem to die. I came to earth to die. I am not going to turn back! I am on the trail of the Divine purpose." And He stayed there! One day He hung on the cross in agony and blood. After awhile He cried, "It is finished." He stayed on the trail. He never got off. He said, "I came to do My Father's will, and now it is done." He died for us. And my Bible says, "He shall see of the travail of His soul, and shall be satisfied."

You will never be happy off the trail. A man that is called of God to preach may do something else. He may go to Congress. He may be a Governor. He may be a United States Senator. He may be a President! But no man was ever happy who left the possum trail of God's purpose. You stay on the trail and do the will of God, or you will never be happy in this world. There is no such thing as contentment and happiness outside the will of God. And there is nothing that can be done to you that will take out of your heart the joy of living as long as you are on the "possum trail" of the Divine purpose.

Stay on the trail! Don't get off of it! Don't you let some little, frizzly-headed, rabbit of a girl stop you until you finish your preparation for the work to which God has called you. The call to preach carries with it a sacred obligation to prepare. You have no right to be a little, shabby, good-for-nothing preacher when you can be a good preacher. You would have contempt for a doctor who would go out to practice medicine unprepared. Yet we fill some of our pulpits with unprepared preachers. Dealing with spiritual matters and immortal souls is far more important than dealing with the bodies of men and pouring medicine down the throats of sick people! You are supposed to finish your educational preparation for the work of the Lord Jesus Christ, the work to which He has called you.

There are some of you girls who are called to be teachers. You are Christian girls. You have a sacred calling. You have no right to stop short of the best preparation it is possible for you to get. Some girl here this morning is called to be a missionary. You have no right to go out unprepared. I've known God to use people who never had a chance to prepare for God's work, but I have never known God to use a person who had a chance and would not take it, or who could have made a chance and would not do it. God won't use you if you let a rabbit divert you from the "possum trail." God doesn't have much use for rabbit-chasers. God likes the folks who stick to the business to which He has called them.

I told you one time when I spoke on the text: "He that wavereth is like a wave of the sea driven with the wind and tossed," that God never trusts a wavering man. A double-minded man is unstable in all his ways. God won't trust a wavering man, the devil won't trust him. So the man who wavers is in a bad fix. I know some men who cannot be trusted. Men can't trust them. God can't trust them. The devil can't trust

them. Nobody can trust them! I am talking to somebody today who, if you walked up and said, "O God,
give me wisdom," God would say, "If I gave it to you
somebody would talk you out of it when you go uptown." You pray, "O God, lead me to what Thou
wouldst have me to do." God says, "No need to pay
any attention to him. If I told him what to do he
would let the devil stop him. He would run into the
devil. The devil would say, 'I wouldn't do it.' He
would talk him over on his side."

Some people are always being talked over by the
devil and then pulled back by God. The devil gets
them and then God gets them again. They never get
anywhere. Instead of running down the road of the
possum trail, they are on the side with God, then on the
side with the devil, then back again on the side with
God. They do all their walking *across* the trail. They
wear themselves out; they run their legs off running
between God and the devil. They are over with the
devil and God says, "Come back." They come back
and say, "All right, God, we are back." The devil says,
"Come over here." They say, "All right," and go back.
Then they say, "We are going to call on God a minute.
now, we will be back in a little while." They just keep
running between God and the devil.

Oh, isn't it wonderful to see a person stay on the
trail? You say to him, "Where are you going?" He
says, "I am going after a possum. I am never going to
stop until I tree him if I have to run a hundred years.
I'll die on the trail." I would rather see a dog die on
the possum trail and never catch a possum than to see
him run off after a rabbit and catch the rabbit. I have
more respect for the dog that runs at night until his

tongue hangs out and until he slobbers himself nearly to death and yet never gets a possum than I do for a dog that runs off after rabbits. If he comes home the next morning with his tail between his legs and says, "I couldn't catch him. He outran me. But I never did turn back; I did the best I could," I will take that old dog in my kitchen and give him a pone of corn bread. I will butter the bread, too! I will wrap him up and hug him and say, "You good old dog! There is one good thing about you, dog; you couldn't be turned back after you got on the trail!"

Some of us will never have our dreams come true— not in this world. Some of us are going to die on the possum trail without ever getting the possum up a tree. After awhile people will come in and say, "Poor old dog! But he never did stop!" Say, listen! if you stay on the trail until you die and don't tree your possum in this world, you will find a possum up a tree in heaven some day. God Almighty won't let you be defeated! And God won't let rabbit-chasers win. God doesn't condone rabbit chasing. He likes possum dogs. What are you? What kind of dog are you? Are you a rabbit-chaser or a possum dog?

If I were going to chase a rabbit I would pick a big one. I would stop and smell. If he smelled like a little one, I would let him go. I can understand a fellow who gets off the possum trail for a hundred million dollars. But I don't understand the fellow who gets off for a hundred dollars a month. The devil doesn't have to pay much to get some people. They sell themselves so cheaply. If the devil were going to get me, he certainly would have to pay a good price, because I want to be a possum dog.

If you, by getting off the possum trail for your life, could get all the money in the United States, all the money in Great Britain, all the wealth of China (and there is wealth in China), all the wealth of Russia (and there is wealth in Russia),—if you could get all the wealth of the world—and yet should wind up without the will of God having been done in your life, you would be a fool! Yet some people in this country leave the possum trail of God Almighty's purpose who will never tree any gold or silver or any of the luxuries of life.

If you could, by getting off the trail of God's purpose for your life, become the Governor of a state, then become a United States Senator, then become the President of the United States, then form a federation of world governments and become the monarch of the world, you would still be a fool!

If you, by getting off the possum trail of God's purpose for your life, could get in society and become the social queen of America and of the world; if you could be written up in the papers as the best-dressed woman or the most charming society woman of the earth and should wind up without God's will having been done in your life, you would be a fool! We have girls in this country who spend their lives chasing little rabbits of pleasure. They always wind up miserable failures. I wouldn't chase little rabbits. If I were going after a rabbit I certainly would stop and take a good smell. I would try to find out the size of the rabbit before I left the possum trail of God's purpose for my life.

Did you ever hear a dog that has treed a possum, bark? Oh, the music! A dog may be a common cur dog. He may have the mange. He may not have any ancestors. He may have ordinary dog blood in him. But let him get a possum up a tree on a cold night and you will hear such music as you have never heard before. He gets a song in his throat. He says, "Come on! Come on! I've got him up a tree! Come on, see what I've done!" You get there and see the dog looking up. He says, "You go up the tree and get him; I can't climb the tree." The possum's eyes shine through the branches of the tree. The dog says, "Go up there and get him or cut the tree down and let me get him!"

The possum is gotten out of the tree and you and your dog start home together. You say to the dog, "What kind of trail did you come over?" Wagging his tail he seems to say, "I have forgotten the trail. I know I came through mud and swam a creek. I must have some blood on me, but I hadn't thought about it." You ask, "Are you sorry you did it?" The dog looks up into your eyes and seems to say, "Me sorry! Oh, boy, not me! I wouldn't have every rabbit in the woods. I love possum! I chased this one. It was a wonderful chase, and at last I won!"

Wait until you hear the old saints of God barking up the tree, the saints who found what God wanted them to do and then would not be turned aside, the saints who stayed on the "possum trail" of the Divine purpose until one day they treed the possum and their hearts began to sing. They will say, "I have finished the course!" They will forget the hardships. They will forget the difficulties. They won't even remember the battles!

I used to go up and hug the old possum-hunting dog. I would say, "You good old dog! I am glad you didn't run off after that rabbit! Come on now, we will go home and get you something to eat." The dog would walk along with us and I would stop and pat him on the head.

If you will stay on the trail of God's purpose for your life, you will get a pat on the head some day, too. It will be the pat of the nail-pierced hand. And you will hear a good voice. It will be Somebody saying, "Well done! Well done! Well done, thou good and faithful servant! Well done!" That one utterance from the lips of our Lord and Master will more than compensate for all the hardships, all the battles, all the struggles, all the brier patches, all the creeks, all the cold nights, all the suffering!

There is really a lot of fun in the chase, too. God is so wonderful! He pays something in advance before we get into the race; He gives us joy on the chase; and then when we have finished He takes us home and rewards us.

Young people, make up your mind whether you are going to be a possum dog or a rabbit-chaser. Make up your mind! Every one of you will be one or the other. Some of you have been smelling a rabbit the last few days. You have been trying to decide whether you will stay on the possum trail or go after the rabbit. Make up your mind and let us know whether you will be back next semester. Any of you rabbit-chasers who are going to start on the chase, let us know right away. Are you going through, or are you going off on a rabbit trail? Are you going to keep step with God and God's purpose, or are you going to run off on a side line? Are you going to be a possum dog or a rabbit-chaser? Make up your mind!

Prayer: "Our Heavenly Father, we thank Thee for the men through the ages who stayed on the trail. We thank Thee for Paul. We thank Thee for the other apostles. Some of them wavered. Some of them got off of the trail once in a while; but, thank God, they came back. We know it is bad to get off. It is worse to stay off. Thou hast a plan for every life here. There is a possum trail of Divine purpose for everybody in this building. Help us to get on that trail and stay on it. Help us never to turn aside until we tree the possum. Help us to go through with God. We beg it in His name! Amen."

The Secret of Success

I AM speaking to you this morning on the subject, "The Secret of Success."

Some time ago I met a very influential, prominent man who had had a wide experience. I asked him if he didn't find that most of the people he met were mediocre? He said, "No, Sir, I do not. They are not even mediocre." The man was right.

Did you ever stop to think how few people in this world succeed? There are many lawyers in this country. How many do you know who are really outstanding in their profession?

Consider the physicians you know. How many of them are outstanding? You can count on the fingers of your hands the great physicians of America.

How many preachers do you know in America who stand out in the ministry? There are a great many good men in the ministry and the Lord is blessing a great many men in the ministry, but you can count on the fingers of your hands the great, well-known preachers of America.

There are a great many people in the educational business and they write a great many books; but how few names of great educators you know in this nation.

If you stop to think about it, you will realize that most of the people you meet are hardly mediocre. Very few people in this world, even from a human standpoint, attain to what we call success. But I have a little theory of life. I believe that the average, ordinary person in this world can succeed.

You young people hear a great deal about the wonderful day in which you are living. It is a day of opportunity, and you have privileges that your grandparents never even dreamed of. But you have problems, too. You are living in a very difficult age. The world is very much keyed up.

A man was talking about the difference between this day and the old days. He said that in the old days a fellow would go to see his girl and there would be a fire in one end of the living room and an old grandpa clock in the corner. The old clock would say, "Take—your—time. Take—your—time. Take—your—time." Now, when a young man goes to see his girl the fire is in the pipe and the light is in the bottle. A little clock on the mantel says, "Get together quick! Get together quick! Get together quick!"

The world is moving. The world is moving as it never has moved before. Everything is keyed up. People are born in a hurry. They live in a hurry and they die by medical aid. The world is keyed up. Things are moving fast.

I remember how my father used to tell about the Civil War and about battles that were fought in those days. To load a gun a soldier would get down in a trench and push the bullet and the wadding down the barrel. The officer would say, "Ready! Fire!" The soldiers would fire and then "duck." Think about war like that. In modern warfare a fellow just lifts the lid of hell, drops tons of explosives, and blows up a city. How the world is moving!

And I want to do a little prophesying. When this war is over, things are going to move as they have never moved before. Missionaries will go to mission fields in planes. The world is going to be keyed up as it has never been keyed up before. We will have modulated frequency radios after the war. Those radios, I understand, have no static—praise the Lord! We have not touched with the tips of our fingers the marvelous possibilities of science. People in this country are talking about electronics. I don't know what they are talking about. It must be something that is going to help move the world faster, though, because everything moves fast! But in this world that is all keyed up, that is wild with excitement, that is moving like lightning, you can have success.

You can have success regardless of the blood in your veins. I have known some people to make good who had poor blood in them. I have known some people to fail with good blood in them. I saw a man one time who was the son of a noble father and wonderful mother, a man whose maternal and paternal grandparents were outstanding, lovely, refined, Christian people, but who himself was one of the "bumiest bums" I ever saw. He was struggling down the road of life, dirty and ragged. Yet he was born in a good home and, everybody said, had good blood in him. You can succeed with poor blood in you and fail with good blood in you.

As a matter of fact, we have this ancestry business turned around. I ran into a fellow not long ago who told me about his ancestors. He went back and back and back! The further back he went, the better his ancestors were. The further they were away from him.

the nicer people they were. His old great grandfather must have been a fine man. I felt it was fortunate that he was dead so he wouldn't have to admit the man was his great grandson. I have known people to talk about where they had come from when they hadn't gone far. It isn't necessary for a person to tell where he came from if he has really gone somewhere. The world finds out where a man came from if he has "gone places."

Years ago in one of our southern states a man advertised in a newspaper that he wanted to buy a buggy horse. On Monday morning a colored man came to see him and said, "Boss, I seed in the paper where you wanted to buy a horse." The man said, "Yes. I want to buy a nice buggy horse." The colored man said, "Well, I would like to sell you this one." The man looked over the horse and said, "John, I wouldn't want that horse." The colored man said, "Why not, Boss?" The man said, "He is the ugliest horse I ever saw. I don't want him." The colored man said, "Boss, let me show you what he can do." The horse went down the road like a cannon ball. But the white man looked at him and said again, "I wouldn't have him. Maybe he would make a good race horse, but I don't like his looks. I like nice looking horses." "But," said the colored man, "You can have him for a hundred dollars, Boss. He sho is a good horse." But the man didn't buy him.

A few minutes later another man drove up and said to the fellow wanting a horse, "I understand you want to buy a horse." "Yes, I do," the man replied. "I would like to sell you this one," the other man said. The buyer looked at him, asked the price, and said,

"How does he move?" The horse stepped around a little but didn't do much. However, the man bought him for a hundred dollars.

A little later the colored man went uptown and led his lank, ugly horse across the wagon yard. A race horse man with a trained eye said, "Say, do you want to sell that horse?" The colored man said, "Yessah, Boss." "What will you take for him?" "A hundred dollars, Boss," the colored man replied. The man bought the horse, put him on the race track and cleaned up on everything in the state. The race horse man went to work and made the horse an ancestry. He went to the northern part of the state and found out who the horse's mother was. Nobody had ever heard of her. She was an old scrub of a pony up there in the hills. He found out who the horse's father was. Nobody had ever heard of him either. He found out who his maternal and paternal grandparents were. The man went to work and made that prize-winning horse some ancestors. He planted him a family tree and put limbs on the tree. The horse made all of his ancestors famous.

Young people, if you really "go places" people will hunt up your ancestors. They will say, "She must have had a good mother. He must have had a wonderful father." If you don't "go places" you will reflect on your father and mother even though they are good people. You can succeed or fail in this life regardless of your ancestors.

You can succeed in spite of your environment. We have a good environment in Bob Jones College. Nobody around here smokes cigarettes. Nobody around here drinks whisky. There are no wild parties here.

Bob Jones College is decent and clean. This is a Christian college. Every class is opened with prayer. The school stands for the Word of God. It stands for the old-time religion. It stands for decency, uprightness, and efficiency. But in this atmosphere you can fail. We don't claim to succeed with everybody who comes to Bob Jones College. I should like, though, to tell you in passing that the people who don't succeed here don't succeed anywhere. If you can't make good in Bob Jones College, you can never make good in life. There is more to help you and less to hurt you right here than any place I have ever known. But you can make a failure in your life even in this atmosphere.

Did you ever stop to think that Lucifer organized an army and started a war against God in a perfect environment—the environment of heaven itself? Adam and Eve had a good environment. Somebody has said that they breathed air that came filtered through jungles of roses. They used to go to sleep at night under coverlets of flowers. In the morning they would throw the coverlet of flowers back and listen to the birds sing in the treetops and see God's sunlight as it came through the trees about them. The air was filled with the perfume of flowers and fruit. But they made a mess of things. You can make a mess of life in a good environment.

It is nice to have a good environment, but don't think that is all you need. You must have something inside you as well as something around you if you are to make good in this world. If you are what you ought to be, you can make an environment. If you are fundamentally wrong, an environment will not necessarily make you right.

I will tell you something else. You can succeed in spite of your handicaps. Everybody has a handicap. I never knew a human being in my life who did anything in this world who didn't do it in spite of a handicap. Everybody has sales resistance to overcome if he makes a success in life. *Everybody has something to overcome.*

I have known some girls who were handicapped by beauty. The worst handicap a girl can have is to be extremely good-looking. I was talking one time to a group of high school young people about the danger of good looks. A girl near the front looked as if she were scared nearly to death. She was good-looking. You boys ought to have seen her! I said, "Honey, don't be uneasy. I am not talking about you."

Everybody has a handicap. Some of us have poor mentality. Some of us have poor digestion. Some of us have poor eyesight. Some of us have poor teeth. Some people suffer from headache. Some are nervous.

Did you ever stop to think of the men in the world who have succeeded in spite of environment and in spite of handicaps? Teddy Roosevelt overcame bad health when he was a child. The present President of the United States, crippled by infantile paralysis, went to the White House leaning on a cane. You can succeed if you have the stuff in you, if you are unconquerable. And, by the way, one of the tests of your character is your ability to overcome your difficulties. How much can you stand up against?

Probably the worst handicapped man ever in Ameri·can public life was Benjamin Brewster, one time Attorney General of the United States. He was a brilliant, upright man. After his term of office expired he was practicing law in the city of Philadelphia. One time he was representing a certain corporation in a case. The case dragged for days. Benjamin Brewster matched his brain against the brain of an inferior lawyer. The inferior lawyer for several days chafed under the spell of the brain of Brewster. Then when the inferior lawyer got up to make his speech to the jury he said, "May it please the court, Gentlemen of the Jury, the corporation represented by this attorney is as black as his face." He expected everybody to smile. But nobody smiled.

Poor deformed, scarred, Benjamin Brewster stood up in all the dignity of his noble manhood and said, "May it please the Court, Gentlemen of the Jury, I have been in public life for a long time; and this is the first time anybody has ever called attention to my physical deformity. When I was a little child—and my mother, God bless her, said I was a beautiful child—I was playing one day before an open fireplace with my little sister. My little sister fell into the fire and I leaped to rescue her. When I pulled her out of that fire not a hair of her little head was singed, but when I got out of the fire my face was as black as that man's heart."

That little lawyer was forced to leave Philadelphia after that for lack of prestige and influence. Brewster—scarred, deformed, handicapped, and with a face that men shuddered to look at—succeeded, while men about him without serious handicaps failed. You can succeed in spite of your handicaps.

I will tell you something else you can do. You can succeed in spite of your past. You may not be what God wanted you to be five years ago, but you can from this day on be what God wants you to be from this day on.

You have heard the old story of the man who went to a pottery. While he looked around the potter showed him a beautiful vase. Then he pointed down to a cuspidor and said, "I meant that cuspidor to be a vase, too; but it broke on the wheel. I couldn't make a vase out of it, so I made a cuspidor."

God may have wanted you five years ago to be a beautiful vase. If you broke in God's hands, He can make a cuspidor out of you. I would rather be a cuspidor made by Almighty God and turned out on His wheel than to be the most beautiful vase the devil could ever produce on his wheel. It is nice to be a vase, but everybody can't be vases. It is nice to be the parlor light—to be a gorgeous chandelier. But the back hall light may be more valuable than the parlor light. I owe a greater debt to the hall light than I owe to the light in the parlor. A dim light in a back hall may save a person from breaking his neck. A beautiful parlor light isn't used except when company comes. You can be from this day on what God wants you to be. You can do it!

What is success? Success is not making money. You may make money while you succeed, but making money is not success. You may even succeed and die poor. You may even fail and die rich. There are rich men in the world who are failures. A rich woman who was weeping over her drunken son said to me, "I wish we were back where we started. I wish we were living in that little cottage and my husband were working in that little store in the small town where he used to work. All the money we have hasn't helped us to succeed."

Somebody said of a man, "He is a success; he is making fifty thousand dollars a year." A man can make fifty thousand dollars a year or one hundred thousand dollars a year or even a million dollars a year and still fail!

What is success? Success is not making money. It is not receiving honor. Hitler will die a failure. Mussolini will die a failure. I understand that his son-in-law was shot yesterday. He was flying high sometime ago.

Many a woman who lived her faithful life in a little home unnoticed and unknown and then died and was buried in a lonely graveyard was a success in God's sight.

What is success? *Success is finding out what God wants you to do and then doing it.* God has a will for your life. He wants some of you to be preachers. Some of you He wants to be missionaries. Others of you He wants to be school teachers or secretaries. He may want somebody here to go to Congress. He may want somebody here to fill a little lonely place where you will live and die unnoticed and unknown. God has a will for your life. God has a will about everything that is connected with your life. God has a will about the boy you marry, the girl you have a date with, the courses you take in school this semester. God has a will about how many hours you study. God has a will about what you pay for your clothes. Listen! God, who, according to His Word, numbers the hairs of our heads and marks the sparrow's fall, has a will for your life and a will about everything that concerns your life. Success is finding His will for your life and letting that will be done in and through your life.

Perhaps you say, "How can I find God's will for my life?" Any surrendered person who will go along with God will eventually reach the place God wants him to reach. It never fails. I didn't start out in life to build a college. I started out to go along with God, and this college is here.

One time a poor, struggling son of a widow climbed up in politics to the Legislature and then one day was elected governor of his state. An old neighbor said to him, "How did you get here?" He said, "I started here when I was a little boy." You are starting out now in life. Some day when you get to where God wants you, He may say to you, "You started here when you were faithful in Bob Jones College." If you are not faithful here you will not be faithful anywhere else, not unless you get converted and are changed.

Doing God's will is not only the secret of success, young people, it is also the secret of happiness. Everything that does what God made it to do is happy. Small fish have a rather hard time, as you have no doubt noticed if you ever watched them as they dodged big fish. But it seems to me that they are always enjoying themselves. Did you ever notice a bird sitting on a limb singing a happy song? If you were sitting on a limb which was being blown by the wind, you couldn't sing very well. But the bird says, "Let the limb break. I can fly!" Do you know why the bird sings as he sits on the limb? He sings because he is doing what God made him to do. Put the bird in water and he would die. Put the fish in the air and he wouldn't play; he would die. God made fish for the water and birds for the air. God made you for a certain place, too.

Do you know why Paul could sing in prison? Do you know why he could look at his scarred back and say, "Glory to God"? He could do it because he was in the will of God. He said he was "called to be an apostle of Jesus Christ *through the will of God.*" Do you know why Paul could glory in tribulation?—he did glory in tribulation, and that is going some! A dumb sheep can be a model of patience. A sheep will let her head be cut off without crying about it, but a sheep won't shout when her head is cut off. I have seen the little things let their heads be cut off and not say a word, but I never heard a sheep say "Hallelujah!" and bleat a sweet bleat when she was having her head cut off. A sheep is patient. A horse is gentle. We used to have one that was as gentle as he could be. We could ride his back, ride his neck, hang onto his mane or onto his tail. We could climb all over him. We could hitch him up and he would pull the load. He was gentle, but I never heard him shout when he was being whipped. If we lashed him with a whip he stepped up a little; but he didn't say, "Thank you for lashing me."

I suppose angels rejoice in Heaven. At least, we read that "There is joy in the presence of the angels of God over one sinner that repenteth." But the Bible doesn't say that angels are happy when they are persecuted. Listen, young people! Listen! To glory in tribulation is to soar higher than the wings of angels ever flew! If you are in the will of God you can join the Apostle in glorying in tribulation.

You can succeed. Never mind your ancestors! Never mind your environment! Never mind your handicaps! Never mind your past! You can succeed from this day on!

What is success? It is not making money. It is not climbing the ladder of fame. It is yielding your life to God and doing what God wants you to do. God help us to let Him have His way with us.

Prayer: "Our Father, bless us as we meet the problems of this day. Consecrate us to the work that is ahead of us. Help us to be true. And may every student in this building this morning be completely yielded to Thee that Thy will may be done in every life here. We ask it in Thy name. Amen."

Fundamental Elements of Success

"And Jesus entered and passed through Jericho.

"And, behold, there was a man named Zacchæus, which was the chief among the publicans, and he was rich.

"And he sought to see Jesus who He was; and could not for the press, because he was little of stature.

"And he ran before, and climbed up into a sycomore tree to see Him; for He was to pass that way.

"And when Jesus came to the place, He looked up, and saw him, and said unto him, Zacchæus, make haste, and come down; for today I must abide at thy house.

"And he made haste, and came down, and received Him joyfully.

"And when they saw it, they all murmured, saying, That He was gone to be guest with a man that is a sinner.

"And Zacchæus stood, and said unto the Lord; Behold, Lord, the half of my goods I give to the poor; and if I have taken any thing from any man by false accusation, I restore him fourfold.

"And Jesus said unto him, This day is salvation come to this house, forsomuch as he also is a son of Abraham.

"For the Son of Man is come to seek and to save that which was lost.'

I HAVE read from the 1st through the 10th verse of the 19th chapter of Luke. I have an old-time evangelistic sermon which I sometimes preach from this Scripture, but I am not going to preach it this morning. Some of you will remember that one time this year I brought a special message from this same Scripture, but I am not going to bring that message this morning. I have thought of something I should like to say to you before I leave the college today.

It doesn't matter what business a person is in; the
fundamental elements of success are just the same. The
same things that make a preacher successful, from a
human standpoint, make a lawyer successful. The same
things that make a doctor a success, make a merchant
a success. The fundamental principles are the same.
The reason many Christian workers are failures in the
world is that they just do not follow the ordinary laws
that govern success.

Measured by world standards, Zacchaeus was a successful man. He had a good position. He was well-to-
do. He may have been dishonest—the probabilities are
that he was dishonest. But from his standpoint he may
not have been dishonest. It is strange what politicians
will do. I have known a great many politicians who
haven't seemed to have any conscience about some
things which I would think were crooked.

Zacchaeus may have made money by what we would
call crooked methods. He probably did. He didn't say
he had, but when he came down out of the tree he said,
"If I have taken any thing from any man by false
accusation, I restore him fourfold." He may have taken
money fraudulently, but of course he may not have
been crooked. Even if he had been dishonest in his
business, from his standpoint he probably took the
thing for granted. It is strange what people take for
granted in this world.

I heard Russell Conwell lecture on "Acres of Dia-
monds" one time. He said, if I remember rightly, that
he had written biographies of over six hundred million-
aires and that practically every one of them was absolutely honest from his own standpoint; that is, he would
keep his word and pay his debts. From an ordinary,

common, everyday business standpoint, a man ought to be honest and straight. It is a wonderful thing to have people say, "He keeps his word. He pays his debts. He will do what he tells you he will do. If he borrows a book he will return it. If he owes you money, he won't forget to pay it."

Measured by the political standards of his day, Zacchaeus may have been a pretty straight man. Of course he didn't have much reputation among the people. He was what we in the South after the Civil War called a scalawag. We had here in the South after the Civil War two types of people. We had the carpetbaggers— the folks from up North who were down here running the country. Then we had the scalawags, the Southern folks who went over with the carpetbaggers and helped them run the affairs. Southern people didn't like the carpetbaggers, but they literally hated the scalawags.

Zacchaeus was a scalawag. The Roman government was persecuting his people, loading them down with taxes. This scalawag went in with them, held a position under the Roman power, and made money out of his position. He wasn't very popular, but as far as his life was concerned he was probably about as decent as the average politician; and he had in his character the elements that make for success. You can learn something from him.

Did you know that you can learn something even from the devil? I have learned a lot of things from him. It was one time said of an old woman that she never said anything against anybody on earth. The meanest people in the community had been picked on, but she would never say anything against them. After awhile somebody said, "Let's talk about the devil and see what

she will say." They got to talking about the devil and
said to the old woman, "What do you think about
him?" "Well," she said, "I think he is an industrious
old boy!" She was right. You can learn something
from the devil. He is a hustler!

Jesus said, "The children of this world are in their
generation wiser than the children of light." Jesus
looked around at the religionists of His day. He saw
business-men on the alert and politicians on the alert.
He said, "These folks are wiser in their generation than
you are in yours."

You can learn something from Zacchaeus who was
the ringleader of the publicans—the people who were
supposed to be the worst crowd in town. Zacchaeus
never turned back because of handicaps. If you don't
learn to overcome handicaps when you are young, you
will never "go places." Every human being who ever
made good on earth had to learn the lesson that he
must not stop. If you will tell me what it takes to
stop you, I will tell you how much force you have. You
can always judge the force of anything by what it takes
to stop it. You have a hard time stopping a bullet.
Get in front of a bullet and try to stop it. It will stop
you! There is force behind the bullet. You can't make
good without force. You have to learn to go through
with things.

Some of you are wondering how you are going to
get back to school next fall. One person said to me,
"I don't know how I am going to get the money." I
said, "Why, you have until September to get it." Anybody in this country who has anything to him can get
the money now. If you can't get it now, you will starve
when this war is over. Money is hanging on trees now.

What does it take to stop you? Some people get a sore toe, or get a headache—any little thing—and they stop! Listen, if any man who ever lived had an excuse to stop, Zacchaeus had an excuse. The little runt! There he was in a big crowd. People looked down on him with contempt. They would say, "There is that old scalawag. Look at him!" Did he say, "Well, I'd like to see Him but I just can't"? He didn't say it! That little scalawag said, "I came uptown to get the bacon. I am going to get the bacon and take it home with me!"

What did he do? He cut the corners, ran down an alley, ducked around people. He made a chariot out of his difficulty and drove past the crowd! He really had an advantage. What looked like a disadvantage was an advantage. He could get between the people. He was like a little kid who could run through people's legs. There are some advantages about being little. You can get through holes that other people can't get through. You can get around and get places. You are not handicapped with overweight. There are some advantages in not having much sense—people don't expect much of you. If you do anything they say, "He turned out so well for the little sense he had." It is wonderful to surprise people, to have them say, "Well, I never thought he would amount to anything."

Zacchaeus, the man who had the poorest chance, got the best seat. He couldn't be stopped. The crowd couldn't stop him. The scorn couldn't stop him! The hisses couldn't stop him! His physical handicaps couldn't stop him! *I salute the little scalawag!* There is something about that kind of fellow that just tickles me to death—the kind of fellow who just won't stop, who just will not give up!

I think our modern system of education has made a lot of folks give up. When I was a boy in school, people never worked problems for us. We had to work them ourselves. I have spit by the hour on an old slate and rubbed it, and worked problems over. Now mama works them, daddy works them, sister works them, Aunt Sally works them, Uncle Henry works them, grandpa works them, grandma works them, the teacher works them. If they don't work them, they are not worked.

• Zacchaeus was a success because he couldn't be stopped. His brakes just wouldn't work. He had a good motor, too; he could take the hill as well as go down-grade. Say, can you take the hills? Zacchaeus was a climber. You say, "My legs are short." So were his! You say, "Circumstances are against me." So were they against Zacchaeus. But he didn't look at circumstances—he got there!

Another thing about Zacchaeus was that he got there on time. Now, listen to me! I have never in my life known a man to be a success who wouldn't get to places on time. If you don't learn to get to places on time, you might as well check yourself off. There isn't a man on American dirt who is a success who didn't learn to get there on time. The world is filled with adult babies. Somebody has to fill their bottles, stick the nipple in their mouths, and then hold the bottle for them. They have to be carried around.

Zacchaeus didn't only get there on time, he got there ahead of time. He was sitting on a limb when the crowd passed—sitting there swinging his legs and watching. I don't blame Jesus for going home with him. I should like to go home with a fellow like that myself. I'll venture the assertion that dinner was on time at his home. If he had had a wife who didn't have meals on time he would have made it hot for her. I will venture the assertion that his home was run right. Boys, let me tell you something: God be merciful to your poor, miserable soul if you marry a lazy, loafing woman!

I can see Jesus coming. I think He must have looked up and said, "Come on down, Zacchaeus, I am going to eat dinner with you today." If Jesus was hungry He knew He could get a good meal and get it on time. I have been invited out to places for lunch at twelve-thirty and have sat there until one-thirty without lunch being ready. By that time I was so mad I couldn't eat. There is nothing that makes me so mad as to have a meal late.

Do you know why Zacchaeus' name is in Holy Writ? He got there on time. He was there when something was doing. If he had been twenty minutes late you never would have heard of him. Your name will never be written down in the book of success if you don't learn to get there on time. Did you ever stop to think how few people have ever been heard of?

The Scripture doesn't say Zacchaeus was brilliant. It doesn't say he was a university graduate. It doesn't say he ever had a lesson in music. (If he ever took piano, he practiced!) It doesn't say that he studied Greek and Hebrew and Latin and German and French. It says he climbed a tree when nobody expected him to do it. You can go to heaven—you can stay in bed and go to heaven. An invalid can go to heaven. You can crawl on your knees to heaven. But there are a lot of folks going to heaven who—if they don't change—

will have to be waited on when they get there. But let me tell you something! You can't walk the highway with the King of kings on this earth and feast in a home with the Son of God and write a record of success if you don't learn to get there on time. I never knew a Bob Jones College preacher boy who always got his papers in late to make a success in life. When I was a boy we called a fellow who was late the "cow's tail." It is the cow's head that gets into the trough and gets the food. The folks who drag behind in life never taste the food of success in this world.

Another thing that made Zacchaeus a success was the fact that he wanted to know what was going on. He had curiosity. He went to see who Jesus was. He didn't know who He was. He just saw a crowd in town and knew something was going on. People get up here and make announcements in chapel and some of you never hear them. You say, "I didn't hear that." If Zacchaeus had been in this house he would know every announcement that has been made this year—and he would have had to have some memory! He wouldn't have missed a thing. He would have listened. If basketball practice had been announced he would have been there. If someone had asked to see him in front of the ticket-window after chapel, he would have been there. If his name had been on a list he would have said, "*Here*". He had a wholesome curiosity.

There is nothing wrong with curiosity. I want to know what is going on. I am alive, and I want to know if there is anything going on in town. I never saw a parade in my life but that I wanted to know what it was. Some people are just not interested. They just have no interest. They are on hand at mealtime so they can stuff. They are looking for a place to sit down, a place to sleep. Outside of eating and sleeping and sitting, they have no interests in life.

Zacchaeus was alert. Are you interested in what is going on? Listen! If I were a student in Bob Jones College, I would not be here ninety days until I knew everything about the college. I would know whom every teacher married; and the ones who were not married I would wonder about—I would wonder if they were ever going to get anybody!

Zacchaeus had energy. He was a good runner. He outran the kids. There wasn't a child in Jericho more energetic than Zacchaeus. Energy! Do you know what energy is? Energy is dynamite, power, high explosive, T. N. T., Nitroglycerin—that driving something that gets in a fellow and won't let him sit down!

Another thing about Zacchaeus was that he was always in the right place. He would have known his seat in chapel. He would never have got embarrassed for getting in some other person's place. He didn't have a comfortable seat—he was on a limb. But he wasn't interested in comfort.

I never saw a man in my life who was interested in his own comfort who ever amounted to anything. Watch him! The man who is concerned most about where he is going to sleep and the sort of chair he is going to sit in—the man with whom that is the big thing in life never goes places. Zacchaeus forgot he was on a limb. He thought he was in a rocking chair. He got so lost in enthusiasm as he sat there swinging that he thought somebody was rocking him! But he was going to have an experience.

"I want a comfortable room, a nice place—everything exactly right," you say. It is nice to have those things, but the fellow who always knows what he is eating never amounts to anything. The fellow who knows exactly how he is eating never amounts to anything. Emerson said in substance, "A great man doesn't know how he eats." A man consumed with a passion to achieve is not always thinking about what he is eating. Did you ever eat a meal and after it was over not know what you had eaten? I have eaten many a meal like that—and I like good eating! When I have something on my mind and heart and have something to do, when I am starting on a road to climb a tree, one thing is just about as good as another. When I am relaxed and resting, when I have nothing especially on my mind then I know what is being served. The reason all this luxurious crowd never amount to anything is that all they are interested in is the middle part of their anatomy—and they usually show more there than anywhere else!

Zacchaeus wasn't concerned about where he was sitting. He was concerned about what he was going to see. Young people, listen—listen! If you make a failure in life, don't "pass the buck" by saying that you never had a chance. Don't say, "I never have a chance;" just say you are no good. If Zacchaeus by his own dynamic driving power got to Jesus, you who have got to Jesus by the grace of God, can go places for Jesus Christ by the power of God working in your lives. Don't be mediocre! Be the best man and the best woman you can be for the glory of God!

People say, "Oh, to be nothing, to be nothing!" Some of them don't have to make any effort to be nothing! They say, "I am a poor worm of the dust." I am not! I am a sinner saved by grace, but I am saved. I am a child of God! It isn't yet manifest what I am going to be, but I am going to see Him some day and be like Him. While I am waiting for that day I am going to hustle.

I want to ask you this question before we go: who had the best time in Jericho that day? Do you think it was the fellow who when he went home and was asked, "Did you see the prominent person?" answered, "No, I didn't get to see him. There was such a big crowd. I just didn't feel like making the effort. It was rather hot, and I didn't feel so very well this morning; so I decided I wouldn't try. I wish I could have seen him. He must have been a very interesting personality." No! While he was saying that, Zacchaeus was saying to Jesus, "Have another biscuit." He was saying, "Bring my Lord something else to eat. Get it hot and have it ready."

Say, it is wonderful to get there! You get there! You can do it if you will. You are a Christian, aren't you? You have God to help you. You go places!

Prayer: "Our Heavenly Father, save us from being loafers. Save us from being no account. Save us from inferiority complexes. Save us from the big head. Help us to be what we ought to be. Help us to know that God's grace saves us and His grace is sufficient for any crisis or temptation through which we may have to go. Help us to know He is stronger than our handicaps and more powerful than our infirmities. Help us to know that with God's omnipotence back of us, if we are willing to be yielded to Him and are willing to do what we ought to do, we can achieve, we can accomplish and do things for God. Save us from being failures here in Bob Jones College. Help these students from now until the close of the school year to do everything they do to the very best of their ability so when commencement comes they can go home and look their mothers and fathers in the face with clear consciences. Help them to be able to look up into Thy face and say, 'God, with the handicaps and the inability, I did the best I could.' If they can honestly say that we know Thou wilt say, 'Well done, thou good and faithful servant.' Help us to be faithful and true in every little thing in life! We ask it for Jesus' sake. Amen."

Big Head or Inferiority Complex

I WANT to talk to you in a practical way about something that concerns all you students here. I thought about it yesterday after having a conversation with one of our students.

There isn't a person in the world who doesn't have something wrong with him. There isn't a perfect physical specimen on earth. There isn't a person here today who doesn't have something wrong with him. You have a bad eye. You don't hear well in one ear. You have a corn on your toe. You don't sleep well at night. Your pillow isn't exactly right; your ear doesn't fit it. There is something wrong with nearly all of you. Some of us are too fat. Some are too thin. Some of us have poor memories. Some of us have memories that in a way are really too good for our reasoning faculties. You will never meet a person who is absolutely balanced. You needn't expect to find that kind of person. The only person in all history who was perfectly balanced was the Lord Jesus Christ. He was the Son of God.

Moses was a great man, but he was impulsive. He got ahead of God and killed a fellow.

Abraham was a man who believed God and went out under God's orders to become the father of a race, but Abraham wasn't perfect. Abraham, as good and great as he was, did not tell the truth one time.

139

The Apostle Paul was not perfect. He had some kind of thorn in his flesh; something was the matter with him.

Did you know that many of our diseases, mental and emotional, are curable by natural processes? I believe in the supernatural. I wouldn't want to live in a universe where there was no supernatural element. But that which is natural and normal comes from God just as the supernatural does. The God who sent His Son to die on a cross and who saves us by His Grace is the same God who sends the sunshine. If you are pale and sallow from living indoors, don't ask God to make roses bloom in your cheeks. Get out in the sunshine and let God's sunshine do it. That is God doing it. It doesn't matter whether God works a miracle or whether He does it through sunshine and fresh air. It is all from God.

A man was preaching a sermon one time about the waters of the Red Sea being driven back so the children of Israel could go through. Somebody said, "Well, that was the natural wind that came along and did it." Somebody else said, "Well, even if the wind did it, God got the wind there at the same time He got His people there." God harnesses the universe to work along with you if you are surrendered to Him.

Most of your troubles are curable by natural processes. I want everybody here to listen to me. I don't want you to misunderstand me. I believe that in your heart every student in this school is a Christian. Some of you may be bluffing; you may be four-flushing. But I think if I asked you this morning whether you are trusting Jesus Christ as your Saviour, every person in this house would stand up and say, "Yes." If you are trusting Him, you are a Christian. Yet all of us know there is something wrong with us.

I find that one of two things is wrong with most people. If one of these two things is not wrong with you—if you don't have one of these diseases, you at least have an inclination toward it. You have a predisposition toward one of these diseases.

Some of you have a predisposition to be an egomaniac. The Bible recognizes that. God tells you not to think of yourself more highly than you ought to think. You are not so tremendously important. Did you know that if you were to die today you wouldn't be missed? Oh, you would break up school for a day or two, for we would have to be respectful! In my lifetime I have seen many a man die whom nobody knew how to get along without, and yet somehow or other things went right on. The world just kept moving.

Young people, I meet many people along life's way who are failures because they overemphasize their own importance. That is the temptation of talented people. The fact that you have talents does not mean you are brilliant. Some people with much talent have little reasoning ability. Some people have special gifts for which they deserve no credit whatsoever. They just have the gifts. What credit does a mockingbird deserve for singing? He is just made that way. When a mockingbird sings, he is not strutting his stuff. A peacock struts. He has tail feathers, but he didn't make them. God Almighty bent over heaven and stuck all those feathers in his tail. I know some people who can sing and play and act. That is about all they can do; yet they get to thinking they are wonderful.

Egotism is carefully observed by this administration. We watch all the time the development of this disease. That is one symptom we spend our time looking for. I will let you students in on a secret. Every member of the faculty is instructed to observe that symptom.

Sometimes a young preacher who goes out from Bob Jones College and is blessed of the Lord gets the big head. One came back after having had a degree of success. He seemed to think he was the most wonderful fellow in the world. He learned here what to put in the Gospel gun and learned here how to shoot the gun, and yet he thought it was his gun and his munitions and his shooting. He did not feel that he owed God or anyone else any gratitude.

What have you on this earth you didn't get from somebody else? What are you stuck up about? Do you know what the cure for the big head is? It is to sit down and realize two things: first, anything you have, you got from God; and you are custodian of that gift —a trustee. Then think of somebody else in the world who has something you don't have.

I remember one time in one of my meetings a fellow got up, the ugliest man I ever saw—and I have seen some ugly people in my lifetime! I have seen faces that would draw a blister on a stone wall. But this was the homeliest fellow I ever saw in my life. He got up and said, "I want everybody to pray for me to stay humble." I looked at him and smiled and said to myself, "It seems to me that would be easy for you, brother. Why don't you use your fool head and you would stay humble. Just go look at yourself in the mirror."

I have always found that some other person had something I didn't have. Somebody has abilities superior to mine. Somebody has talents that I do not have. Somebody can do something I can't do. Somebody has been used of God in a way I have never been used. Once in a while I sit down and think it over.

I have had temptations. I started to preach when I was a boy. Every old sister who came up would tell me not to go to college. She would say, "That is the best preaching we have ever heard in this country." Don't pay attention to these old country sisters. They tell all the preachers the same thing. They love the Gospel, and it all sounds good to them. But I learned back in those days that there were other preachers in that country. It was hard for me to realize! But I did realize it. Sit down and use your head and get over the big head.

There is another fault, a disease, that people have a tendency toward. It is the disease of an inferiority complex. There are students in Bob Jones College who are suffering from that. Don't underestimate yourself.

I know what I can do. I know my limitations. I know my resources, too; I ought to know. I am a pretty good executive. But I am a little too soft. If a person goes to crying around me, he can get anything I have. If it weren't for that one thing, I would be a pretty good executive.

There is another thing that I know about myself. I can make people see what I am talking about. I am not an orator, but people usually know what I have said when I say it. That is more than you can say about some orators. I know certain things I can do, and I know certain things I can't do. I can't sing to suit anybody except myself. I know my limitations.

I don't believe there is a student in Bob Jones College this morning who couldn't make good. I told a boy in my office the other day—a fine boy and a Christian boy, suffering from an inferiority complex and developing a morbid attitude toward life because he feels he has certain limitations—"You don't have to take anybody's dust. Straighten up and go on and do business. You have the ability."

Some of you students this morning are tempted to have the big head. Some of you would be a thousand times better off if you would check in on your stock and see what you have on the counters and on the shelves. You can see, can't you? You can hear, can't you? You can get around, can't you? You know how to get around and accomplish things, don't you? Well, don't bluster around to cure an inferiority complex. A lot of people go to strutting to cure it. Some who have an inferiority complex step around on the other side and strut their way through life. That is not the way to do it. Just say, "Well, I can't do everything some other people can do, but I can do what the Lord wants *me* to do." Whatever the Lord wants you to do, you can do. If you are pleasing God you ought to be pretty well satisfied, don't you think?

I had a girl in my office this year. She is taking music. That girl is being all the time irritated in her own heart by ambitions to be a musician. She has certain limitations, but she could be a pretty good musician if she would just go ahead and be herself and quit suffering because she can't do what somebody else can do and because she doesn't get the attention which somebody else gets and which she thinks she ought to have. She is going along through school irritated. I think she has improved, but the main thing wrong with that girl is an inferiority complex. She is bluffing her way along. Some people think she has the big head. She doesn't have the big head at all. It is the other kind of disease she has—an inferiority complex.

Now, let me tell you something. You look fairly well. You are not so terrible looking. I wouldn't call you handsome. I wouldn't say that if I were a girl I would fall for any of you boys. Most of you girls here today look fairly well. But then that doesn't make any difference anyway. The homely ones get married the same as the good-looking ones. I have known girls who weren't good-looking. They just didn't look good; but, boy, they had sort of a personality! You could develop that if you would wake up. It is sometimes wonderful how a girl can wake up and develop personality. Use your head! Don't be discouraged because somebody took him away from you. There are other fish in the sea—maybe better than the one you had on the hook and lost. You tried to pull him in and somebody else grabbed him. Let her have him! Maybe you will get a better one some day.

I know a girl like that. She came to Bob Jones College. She lost her boy friend. It nearly broke her heart. Today her heart would have been broken had she got him. He married another girl and bossed her all over the place. Don't you marry one who wants to run over you all the time!

Now, listen, I am not playing with you, boys and girls. I don't advise you to spend too much time thinking about yourself. Get out of yourself. But if I were you, I would sometimes sit down and check the things I didn't have and the things I did have. I would say, "Well, I don't have what some other people have, but I have this and I can do what the Lord wants me to do. I am going to do it. I am not going to have an inferiority complex. I am going to do the best I can."

If I had the big head I would contrast some of the talents other people have with the talents I have and I would get over it.

Your problems, most of them, can be solved by ordinary, natural, mental processes. Adjusting your mental processes will not save your soul, but it will often cure defects in your character. Sometimes a thing like pride, ambition, or egotism has you in such a strong grip—or you are so completely down and out—that the only thing on earth that can pull you up to your feet again is the supernatural miracle-working grace of God. Then God brings a miracle. But most of us in this building today have some little defect in our character that ordinary, practical, common sense would fix if we would go to using it. Let's do it.

Prayer: "Our Heavenly Father, we thank Thee for the fellowship and the glorious opportunities we have here. We thank Thee for our minds. We thank Thee we can hear things that are said to us. We thank Thee that we have an opportunity here to come in touch with the right kind of ideas. We thank Thee for the cultural advantages and for the uplifting influences here. Above all, we thank Thee for Thy grace that saved us. Help us all here to be faithful and true and loyal. Help us to make the most of our lives and to drop off the things we ought to let go. Save us from being egotists. Save us from inferiority complexes. Help us in this time when the world needs Christian leadership so much to be as well-balanced and as normal as it is possible for Christian young people to be. Supply our needs. Build us up where we are weak and give us the strength for the tasks and the responsibilities we have today. We ask it in the name of Jesus Christ our Lord. Amen."

Traffic Blocked

WHILE reading my Bible on the train recently, I found the little text to which I wish to call your attention this morning. No doubt I had read the text before, but I never really saw it until that day. It is a great text—so great that it almost knocked me out of my seat on the train. It is found in the 14th verse of the 59th chapter of Isaiah, just a little clause in that verse: "Truth is fallen in the street and equity cannot enter." In other words, truth is fallen in the street, traffic is blocked, and that which is right cannot pass.

The text does not say that truth is dead in the street. It says that truth has *fallen* in the street. Truth is just inactive. Young people, truth can never be destroyed. Truth is eternal. Truth was born with God and will end when God ends, and God is from everlasting to everlasting. Truth never dies. It doesn't die a natural death, and men can't kill it.

Jesus Christ was born of a virgin. That always will be true. Jesus Christ was incarnate. That always will be true. The Ten Commandments came from God. That always will be true. This Bible is inspired. It doesn't matter what men say about it, the Bible is God's inspired Book. That truth can never be destroyed. The Bible always will be God's inspired Word.

"Heaven and earth shall pass away, but My words shall not pass away," said Jesus. You can't destroy truth. Let's get that definitely fixed in our minds and hearts. You can't even, the Bible says, do anything against the truth except to knock it down and block the street. Then it becomes inactive. And when truth is knocked down, or truth lies down, or truth becomes inactive, immediately the traffic of right is blocked.

Take the truth of mathematics. Twice two has always been four. Twice two always will be four. We have addition, subtraction, multiplication, and division. You can stand up until doomsday and say, "Hurrah for mathematics! Hurrah for arithmetic! Glory to God for addition! Hallelujah for subtraction! Amen to the multiplication tables!" But if you don't use mathematics, equitable business traffic stops.

Take the truth of science. You can say, "I am for science. I am for all the scientific discoveries, every one of them. Glory to God for science! Hurrah for laboratories! Blessed be God for bombs that explode! Hurrah for all the scientific research!" But if you quit using science, if you knock it down in the street and quit using scientific discoveries, what happens? Progress stops! Traffic gets blocked. Say, isn't the Bible a sensible Book? Can't God say a great deal in just a few words?

The same thing holds true in the field of religion. What is the matter with the world? What is the matter with our bloody world? Why are we in such a mess? Spiritual progress has been stopped; that is what is the matter. Traffic is blocked because spiritual truth has become inactive. We have built empires on falsehoods and civilizations on lies. Truth has not been destroyed. It cannot be destroyed. But truth is knocked down in the street. The world is bloody. We are in distress and trouble and turmoil and sorrow.

What is the matter with young people in this country? What brought on this wave of sensuality that has swept over America? Why are we having so many juvenile criminals? There is just one reason: truth went to sleep in the home and in the schoolroom. A man said to me not long ago, "You know, Bob, prohibition made all this lawlessness." No, prohibition in America just showed up the lawlessness. It didn't make it; it just revealed it. People kept the prohibition law as well as they keep other laws. This is a lawless generation. Why is it? Well, truth has fallen in the street. In the schoolroom young people have been taught, "Live your own lives. You don't need anybody to tell you what to do. The Bible isn't God's Word anyway. Oh, there may be some of God's Word in it; but we will decide which is God's Word and which is not His Word." The Bible says that what you reap you will sow, but that doesn't make any difference to some people. The Bible says you can't beat the game of sin, but some people think they can. *Truth fell down. Doctors of Philosophy kicked it down. Professors stepped on it. School processions marched over it. Academic gowns dragged in its face.* Now all hell has broken loose! That which was right got blocked at the entrance of the street. The reason is, truth has fallen down.

Young people, you had better build your life on truth. I think Bob, Jr., in his chapel talk yesterday morning said something about the sins of fundamentalists. Of course, we at Bob Jones College are fundamentalists. We are very fundamental! I think I told you a certain modernistic preacher called me a fun*damn*mentalist. Somebody else said, "He is a *funny*mentalist." Of course, we are fundamentalists. Of course, this school is fundamental! But there are some men in this country today who are saying, "Hurrah for orthodoxy! Amen for the Bible! Hallelujah for the old-time religion! Glory to God for the faith that was once and for all delivered to the saints! Hurrah! Hurrah!" but who are not doing anything. They don't use their tongues except to say, "Hurrah." You can say "Hurrah" for a fellow who is asleep. You can say, "He is a handsome man when he is asleep. I like his snoring, too—doesn't he snore well?" But what good does that do? If a man should get up, wake him up!

You will find fundamental churches that are empty all over America. You will find fundamental preachers who are doing nothing except to tell people they are for the Bible and, of course, criticize those who do not agree with them. Truth has gone to sleep. When truth goes to sleep or falls down, when it becomes inactive, then equity, spiritual progress and victory, are stopped.

You can't build the right kind of life on falsehood. And you can't build the right kind of life on inactive truth. You had better build your life on the right kind of foundation. The Lord said that some people build their houses on the sand and that when the storms come, the winds blow, and the sea sends lashing waves to the shore, their houses fall. The man who builds his house on a rock is safe. Let the storms come, who cares? Let the winds blow, who cares? Let the sea be lashed to fury, who cares! The house has a good foundation. You must build your life not on just a statement of truth, but on truth that is active.

May God Almighty save Bob Jones College students from just saying an orthodox creed on Sunday and living like the devil the rest of the time. There are folks in America who say their creeds and give a lie to what they say every day they live. That is what is the matter with our churches. Most of them have creeds that are fundamentally sound, but they have chloroformed the truth of those creeds. They have put truth to sleep so they can do as they please and still feel comfortable.

What kind of progress are you making? Has traffic been blocked as far as you are concerned? You have said a creed every morning this year. You say, "I am in an orthodox college." You say, "I believe in God the Father. I believe the Bible is the Word of God, etc.;" but what kind of progress have you made? Do you just say the creed to be saying it? Don't you be a sham and a humbug! If you are not living the right kind of life, then truth is sleeping as far as you are concerned. It has fallen down. If you have no spiritual life, you have chloroformed truth in your heart. When truth is marching and you follow truth, you "go places." Truth leads somewhere!

Young people, you are living in a messy world. This government has chloroformed truth. America isn't a Christian nation. Great Britain says her creeds, too—just talks. Just saying creeds isn't enough. This college is built upon an orthodox foundation, on the Word of God. All over America other colleges have been built on that same foundation. What has happened to some of them? Truth fell down and traffic stopped. Don't you ever run through this college creed just to say it! Don't you ever run through the Lord's

Prayer parrot-like! You can repeat creeds and say prayers until doomsday and never get anywhere. You came to Bob Jones College, an institution that you knew stands for God. How far have you gone? A few students have gone home. They couldn't fit in. They couldn't stand it. They couldn't take it. They couldn't go anywhere. Truth to them was sleeping and they didn't have enough energy to wake it up.

I have seen old, gray-headed men and women in America who had made no spiritual progress for many years. Some of them even went backward. They couldn't go around truth. They didn't want to step on it. So they backed off from truth. They were actually afraid that truth would wake up.

Did you ever see traffic get stopped? A fellow faints and falls down in a crowded street. Folks gather around. The policeman comes up. Somebody asks, "What is the matter! What is the matter! Is the man dead!" Somebody else answers, "No." "Is anybody dead?" "No. A man fainted. He fell down." There is something wrong with a fellow when he falls down. You don't fall down unless there is something wrong with you; you are careless; you are not normal; something trips you or something else happens.

When truth falls down in the street of life, what stops? The thing that is right stops. Equity stops. Honesty stops. Folks go to stealing, lying, living in adultery, and raising hell. What stops? Progress stops. Mother stops to weep. Father stops with a broken heart. Young people stop to reap what they have sown—to reap corruption.

What truth has fallen down in *your* life? It is right to be honest. You know that, don't you? Well, is that truth in your heart a living, vital, dynamic principle, or is it just a creed that you say? It is right to be clean, decent, and pure. You know that, don't you? Well, are purity and decency living, dynamic principles in your life? "Children, obey your parents." That is an order from the God who made you. You know it is right to honor your mother, don't you? You say, "Oh yes, it is in the Bible." Well, do it then!

Young people of Bob Jones College, let us get hold of the principles of truth that have fallen down. Let us shake them into activity. Let us pull them up out of the street and say, "Go on, and we will go with you!"

You will remember this text, won't you? Yes, you will! This will be one of the texts you will always remember. I hope it will do you some good. You say you will remember it, but will it be an active principle in your life? Let us say the text again: *"Truth is fallen in the street and equity cannot enter."* The thing that is right, the equitable thing, can't walk over truth that is inactive. That is the principle. Can you remember that? That which is right cannot go forward over the body of inactive truth.

Prayer: "Our Heavenly Father, we pray Thee that the wonderful truths that we all know may be vital and dynamic and powerful in our lives. Bless us all, we pray. Make these days at Bob Jones College days of spiritual progress, days of victory. May there come upon all of us a strange Divine anointing. Keep us by Thy power for Jesus' sake! Amen."

Feeling Your Way Along

"WE grope for the wall like the blind, and we grope as if we had no eyes; we stumble at noon day as in the night . . ." That is the 10th verse of the 59th chapter of Isaiah.

These words were addressed to Israel while the nation was in a state of apostasy and they have a national application, of course. But, young people, the truths concerning Israel and all truths that have to do with spiritual living, belong to us, too. I knew a minister who would not preach from "The Sermon on the Mount." He said it was to be the inaugural address of the King and that he never preached on it. Some good people never pray the Lord's Prayer. They say it doesn't belong to this dispensation. I haven't much patience with that sort of attitude.

The statement, "The pure in heart shall see God," which is found in "The Sermon on the Mount," is just as true today as it was when Jesus made it. It will be true in the millennial kingdom. It will be true through all eternity. Nobody but the pure in heart can ever see God. That is an eternal truth.

There isn't anything in the Lord's Prayer that I don't want. I want His kingdom to come, don't you? I want daily bread, don't you? I want my sins forgiven, don't you? Some people get so technical that they rob their lives of many spiritual blessings.

This text concerns Israel. We read in the first chapter of Isaiah that the book is "concerning Judah and Jerusalem." But there are many things in the book of Isaiah that are applicable to the church that never were intended directly for the church. All the truths that run through the book of Isaiah, spiritual truths, belong to us, too. We are doing exactly what Israel is accused in the text of doing.

Now think about it. These people had two good eyes and plenty of sunshine. But instead of using their eyes and walking in the light, they were groping along in the darkness. That is exactly what this old world is doing today. That is what the United States Government is doing. When Mr. Roosevelt said, "We have a rendezvous with destiny," he had in mind a sort of feeling-along process. The nations of the world today are not walking in the light. They are not using their eyes. They are feeling their way along. That is the way nine-tenths of the people you see on earth today are living. That is the way some of you are living.

I had a girl in my office yesterday. I was sorry for her. She is a sweet girl, a good girl. But she wanted to do a certain thing that we couldn't endorse. I was sympathetic and took a lot of time with her, but she was trying to argue herself into something and argue me into something that she in her heart knew was contrary to what she should do. That girl was running on feeling. Feeling was her guide—not the thing that was right.

The easiest job you ever had on earth is to find what is right. If you have a grain of sense you can find out what is right about anything. If you don't know, ask somebody. But the hardest job you ever had on earth is to feel your way through life and not get into trouble. That is exactly what some of you have been doing, what all of us have done at some time along the way of life. Almost all the trouble I have ever had in my life has come as the result of letting my feelings be my guide when I had two good eyes and plenty of sunlight. There isn't a student in Bob Jones College who doesn't know what is right. You all know what is right. Listen, if you don't know, you can find out what is right. The trouble with most of us is that we have eyes but won't use them. We have sunlight, but we won't walk in it.

I saw a pathetic thing the other day in Denver, Colorado. A poor, old blind man with a cane in his hand was coming down a sidewalk, feeling his way along. He went up to a door and put his hand on the door. I stopped and said, "Can I do anything for you?" He said, "Is this the hotel?" I said, "Yes, sir." He said, "Thank you. Thank you very much," and felt his way in. Now that is pathetic. But what would people have thought of me, a man with two fairly good eyes, if they had seen me walking down the street on a bright day, feeling my way along? Yet that is exactly the way some people do in life.

Some fellow falls in love with a girl. He is just crazy about her. He always was a little crazy, now he is absolutely crazy! He knows it is not time for him to get married. He has figured it out. He can think. He has judgment. He knows he ought to prepare for life by finishing his education. He has his eyes open— if he hasn't, he will get them open some day! But he feels something in his heart. It feels funny! And he *feels* his way along life's road. Some of you are going through life, guided by your feelings.

Some people run their religion on feeling. Feeling, as far as I know, is never mentioned in the Bible in connection with salvation; and yet most of the people in this country put more emphasis on feeling than they put on the Word of God and on Christian faith., It is all right to be happy. It is wonderful to have the joy of the Lord and the peace of God. Nobody discounts that. But those are not the essential things. The essential thing is the truth in Christianity.

Sam Jones used to say, "Feeling is moral perspiration." In illustration he would say, "Suppose I go down in the field on a cold winter's morning and find a fellow with an ax in his hand and say, 'What are you doing?' The fellow says, 'I am going to cut the tree when I sweat. When I go to sweating, I will cut.'" Sam said he would say, "You old fool, cut the tree and you will sweat. If you will go to cutting, you will go to sweating!"

People so often say, "I don't feel like it. I don't feel like it." What does feeling have to do with it when you have two good eyes and know which way to go? I never feel much like getting up in the morning. The most comfortable feeling in the world is a nice bed early in the morning. Some people say, "I feel too bad to get up." I always feel too *good* to get up. That is the reason I hesitate! But the right thing to do is to get up and begin the day's work.

Suppose a woman says, "Well, I just don't feel like getting up. I am not going to get any meals today. I will let you do the best you can around here today. You can starve to death as far as I am concerned. I don't feel like getting up." Suppose somebody says to her, "But it is your duty," and she answers, "I know it. But feeling is strong with me, and this bed feels good. Let the babies starve, what do I care!" You would say, "Why she is a mean woman!" Well, do you run your life on feeling or do you do under all conditions the thing you know you ought to do? The Lord says the children of Israel were operating on feeling, not on eyesight. They knew the road and they could see, but they went on feeling.

Why don't you use the light that God gives you? Why don't you use good, common sense? I have told you students over and over that God never brings into use the supernatural when the natural will do. If you have sense enough to know what is right, just go on and do it. Just use your head. I have told you so many times that God gave you your head to use. That is what it is up there for. It wasn't put there for decoration. God gave you eyes with which to see. If you bandage them up, you will go blind. Stop up your ears and you will get to where you can't hear. Bandage your arm and you will get to where you can't use it. Fail to use your legs and you will get to where you can't walk. If you don't use the light, after awhile the light will get to where it is useless to you.

If you don't use good, common sense day by day in the decisions of life, after awhile God will take away from you that which you don't use. We read in the Bible about a man who gave a talent to his servant. The servant wrapped in a napkin the talent that was given him and buried it. Later the man returned and took the talent away from him. God takes away from you the things you tie up in a napkin and won't use.

God will take away from you Christian judgment if you don't use it. God will take away from you spiritual eyesight if you don't use it!

That is what happened to the Children of Israel. They had eyesight. They had the prophets. They had the Old Testament. They had God. They were the repository of the truth. Through their loins came the Messiah. Israel that had light refused to use that light and God blinded her eyes. The Jewish race today is scattered over the earth, blind to God's movement and to God's spiritual program. They didn't use their eyes. And if you fail to use what God gives you in the way of spiritual judgment, some day you will not only be blind but you will also be unable even to feel.

When you feel you want to do something, check your feeling against that which is sensible and right. If your feelings are contrary to the light, then follow the light. When feelings and light go arm in arm down the street, it is all right. But when feelings prove you are in a dark alley groping your way along, you had better watch out. Young people, there is only one question for you to ask about anything. That question is: What is right?

Last year I was convinced that it would be wrong for us to take out time for Christmas holidays. I was convinced it would be wrong to take two weeks in a busy, bloody world and send young folks up and down this country on trains in congested traffic. We all felt that we wanted a Christmas vacation. But I was convinced it would be wrong to take it. The more I thought about it, the more I was convinced. The students were convinced, too; and we decided on the basis of right. We decided to stay here, and we had the best Christmas we have ever had. I have tried to make all my decisions, especially in recent years, on the basis of what is right and not on the basis of how I feel. I know if I do that I shall never have to worry about anything. If you will about any matter just ask one question: "Is this right?" and then act on the honest answer to that question, it will turn out all right in the end.

Recently a fine Christian young lady asked, "Should I get married?" She asked the right question. The question should not be, "Do I want to get married?" The question should be, *"Should* I get married?" I asked her if the young man she was considering marrying were a Christian. The Bible says that a Christian is not to be unequally yoked together with an unbeliever. You as a Christian have no right to get married if the person to whom you are to be married is an unsaved person.

Sometimes a student asks, "Should I quit school? Should I throw up my hands and give up? I *feel* like quitting. I could get a job. There is good money to be had now. What should I do?" The question should be: "What is right?" And if you want to know, just open your eyes and see. You don't have to go stumbling in the night.

Let me tell you who have come to Bob Jones College something: if you stay in the light of this place and do not keep your eyes open and do not go in the right way, there isn't much hope for you. If you don't make good in Bob Jones College you won't make good. I am not talking about a brilliant record in books; but if you don't make good in Bob Jones College, you won't make good anywhere. Oh, you may seem to make good, but you won't make good out in the world. You may get a job. Anybody can get a job now. You don't have to have any ability to get a job. You ought to see the folks I find working. You ought to sit down at the average lunch counter or in the average hotel today and see the kind of waitresses you would have. You ought to see the kind of service people get. Don't think you are making good; don't pat yourself on the back and think you are somebody because you can get a job under war conditions. Anybody can get a job now. People will hire petticoats and pants—anything under war conditions. It is no trouble to make money now—$25, $30, $40, or $50 a week. But wait until hard days come and see how you come out then.

I don't care how much light you have, how good your eyes are, or how much your eyes are open, you will always have fallible judgment. You will sometimes fall down on the right road and in the light of noonday. You won't always go along without stumbling. You will trip on an orange peeling, or something will happen. But if I were you I would use the light I had. I wouldn't shut my eyes at noonday. Your eyes are supposed to be open when it is light and I wouldn't feel for a wall when I had two good eyes with which to see and two good legs on which to walk. In the first place, that is slow progress. You don't get anywhere that way.

Israel had light but didn't use it. Where are her people now? Some of them are driving fruit wagons. Some of the fellows you see in America driving fruit wagons are descendants of Israel's religious leaders. Some of them are descendants of the old Solomon days. Others are being kicked around in Germany, killed in

Poland, and eaten up with lice in prison camps! What is the matter with them? The same thing that is the matter with Rome. The people of Rome didn't walk in the light. The same thing that happened to Greece. Greece in her glory didn't have all the light we have, but she did have the light of philosophy. The people of Greece did have a man who talked about an unknown God and told them about Him. But they turned from the light they had.

You had better walk in the light you are getting here. If you don't, you will find yourselves in darkness. You will be where you can't see. You will grope as blind men grope for a wall and stumble at the noonday as folks stumble in the dark.

Don't blame the Jews for stumbling today. Blame Israel for not walking in the light two thousand years ago when her people said, "His blood be on us, and on our children." I don't blame the hopeless, miserable dope fiend with needle points all over his body who drags his poor, ruined body out of the dive and staggers down the street. I blame him for not using his eyes back yonder when he knew that dope would ruin him. Don't blame sinners for being in the ditch. Blame them for getting into the ditch.

Any person in this country knows nicotine is bad for him. If cigarettes keep a fellow from playing good football, he should not smoke cigarettes. A girl who will smoke cigarettes and drink liquor is a fool. Anybody who will pour nicotine into his blood and his glands is just a fool. These young people who hang around saloons drinking liquor are just shutting their eyes. They know better. They have studied physiology. These young girls in this country who are playing a loose game on the highway of life, know better. God put in the soul of a girl an instinctive something that draws her back from that which isn't decent.

You young people here at Bob Jones College know what is decent and upright. You have enough sense to come in out of the rain. But there are people in this country who have enough sense to go out of the rain into a shed for protection and yet who go out and expose themselves to all the dangerous storms of immorality.

Quit feeling your way along! Use your eyes! You have good eyes. You know what is right. If you don't know what is right and what is wrong, come to my office and I will tell you. Ask your roommate, maybe he can tell you. Ask your teacher. I think your teacher can tell you. If you don't know what is right, ask somebody. If you don't know how to use spiritual light, find out. Quit feeling along for the wall when you don't have it to do. If you will use the eyes that you have, the light that God has given you, you won't go blind spiritually. Use your eyes—use your spiritual eyes!

Prayer: "Our Father, save us from the tragedy into which multiplied millions of young people are going. Lord, we are flesh and blood and nerves and bones—we are human. The world has something to pull us, something that answers to the law of gravitation that pulls us downward. Help us to know that right living is uphill living and wrong living is going downgrade. Help us to use all the spiritual eyesight we have. Some of us have more than others, just as some of us have better physical eyesight than others. But there is not a person in this auditorium who cannot see spiritually.

Help us to use our eyes! It will be midnight in some of the places these young people are going. But the light shines here. Help us to walk in it! Lord God, save us from the tragedy of going blind, of crying for light and not finding it, and of having to feel our way through the darkness of time and eternity. Make us what we ought to be. Keep us by Thy power. For Jesus' sake. Amen."

Weights and Besetting Sins

"Wherefore seeing we also are compassed about with so great a cloud of witnesses, let us lay aside every weight, and the sin which doth so easily beset us, and let us run with patience the race that is set before us.

"Looking unto Jesus the author and finisher of our faith; who for the joy that was set before Him endured the cross, despising the shame, and is set down at the right hand of the throne of God."

I HAVE read the 1st and 2d verses of the 12th chapter of Hebrews.

Sometime ago I was turning the dial on the radio and accidentally tuned in to a prize fight. There was a good deal of excitement going on and I thought I would listen for a while. I was especially interested in the announcement that there were several ex-champions present at the broadcast. Each one was presented as former champion So-and-so. As they were presented each came to the microphone and said a few words.

Here in this wonderful 12th chapter of Hebrews, God calls the roll of the champions. The champions are at the race. There is a big crowd of them, a great throng. We call them to the microphone. I won't have time to name all of them, but Abraham is here. We ask Abraham, "What about the race?" Abraham says, "You can win it all right. It can be done; I did it." We ask Enoch about it. Enoch says, "I had a walking marathon one day. I walked and walked and walked until I got home. You can do it, too." If I had time I would take them one by one and let each of the former champions tell you how it can be done.

After God names the champions He says, "Now, you are in the race." Remember you have to be a Christian to get in the race, but if you are already a Christian you *are* in the race. And listen! Jesus is your Manager. He has made "the deal" for you. He has arranged for the race. He has mapped out the course for you. He has mapped out a course for your life. He has fixed the race track for you. He has put you on it. He has told you about the champions that have won before.

You have a great crowd of witnesses here. But these witnesses can't do anything for you except to encourage you. All they can do is to tell you it can be done. Enoch, what can you do for them? Enoch answers, "I can't do anything except to tell them what I did and where I got power to do it." Abraham, what can you do? Abraham answers, "I can't do a thing but tell them that I won and tell them how I won. That is all I can do." Well, Abraham, can you impart any power to them? Abraham answers, "I can't do a thing."

Boys and girls, don't play to the grandstand. *Look to Jesus.* Jesus is the only one who can help you. All the saints who have gone on before can only encourage you. All they have achieved can make you feel that it can be done, but they have no power to impart to you. But Jesus can help you. God says you are compassed about by a great cloud of witnesses, but they can't win for you. You have them around you, and it is nice to have them. The grandstand is full of them. They are honored people. But you must put your eyes on Jesus in the race. Young people, you will never win any other way. *There is nobody who can help you except Jesus.*

Now God says, "You have the crowd of witnesses. You have Jesus as your Manager, the Author and Finisher of your faith. He is with you at the beginning. He will go down the race track with you. And He will be at the end of the track waiting for you when you get there." Then He says, "I want you to win this race, and I will tell you how to do it. There are three things you must do: *First, Look to Jesus.* That is essential! Put your eyes on Him! *Second, Lay aside every weight and the sin which doth so easily beset you. Third, Run the race with patience.*

"Lay aside the weight." I don't know whether I am right about this. It may not be taught here, but it is true anyway. A great many people carry weights that are not actual sins. Some people carry the weight of ignorance. There is nothing that weighs a person down more than ignorance. It is not a sin to be ignorant. *But it is a sin to stay ignorant.* It is not a sin to be lazy. *It is a sin to give up to laziness.* You should pep up. You should take an iron tonic. You should breathe some fresh air. Make up your mind—do something about your laziness.

Suppose I should run down a street in this town with a jug of whisky in one hand and a grindstone under the other arm. Suppose I say to myself, "Now, I ought not to have this jug of whisky. It is a sin to carry this jug of liquor. It is wrong. I am going to throw it down." I throw the jug of liquor down. But I have the grindstone. I say, "I will carry the grindstone;

there is nothing wrong with that." The jug of liquor
is a sin. The grindstone is a fault. I drop the sin—
that is a good thing. But sometimes a fault will hold
one down almost as bad as a sin. If the grindstone
keeps you from running successfully, get rid of the
grindstone! If you keep a fault that you know to be a
fault, soon it turns into a sin. Let me say that again.
If you have a fault and know you have it, you should
get rid of it. *Faults turn to sins when people could get
rid of them and won't do it.* If you have the grindstone, throw that down, too. Get rid of everything in
your life that keeps you from winning this race.

A great many people delight themselves in their
faults. A girl said to me one time, "Everybody thinks
I am angry when I am not angry." Well, listen young
lady, if that is so, then it is just the same as far as effect
is concerned as if you were angry. It may not be exactly the same as far as your character is concerned, but
it is just the same in its effect and influence.

Bob, Jr., said to me the other day, "There is bound
to be something wrong with one girl in this college.
She couldn't look as she looks at chapel and be what
she ought to be." I asked, "What do you mean, Bob?"
He said, "I never see her look up. She has a hard, cold,
rebellious look as she sits in chapel. I have watched
her and it doesn't matter who speaks she just looks
down and frowns." Your countenance betrays you,
young lady. If you have a frown that you could get
rid of and you keep it, that frown becomes a sin. If you
have a harshness in your throat that hurts your testimony, take lessons in speech and get rid of it. If you
have a style about you that hurts your testimony, get
rid of it. It is wrong to keep it. You are in Bob Jones

College not only to get rid of your sins but also to get rid of your faults.

Many people hug their faults to them; they nurse their faults and enjoy their faults. They walk around and talk about the wonderful faults they have. They say, "This is my fault." Well, don't brag about it. You are to lay aside the weight as well as the sin that so easily besets you. You ought always to be figuring on what you can get rid of that will help you win the race—what weight you can take off you, what you can unload. Nearly every one of us has something that should be given up.

I have a fault, a serious fault. I am possibly too old to change. I have always talked too fast. Some people in my audience cannot keep up with me when I turn loose in my campaigns. When I was a young fellow I should have had somebody to make me be just a little more deliberate in speech, but not enough to change my individuality and not enough to make me different from what I am naturally. I don't believe in a person's losing his individuality; but with a little coaching I could have got rid of that too rapid speech. A boy came up to me the other day when I was speaking in Boston and said, "I like for you to talk fast. I talk fast too. I like to talk fast; blab, blab, blab!" "Well," I said, "young fellow, you ought to stop it. You are young enough to do it."

Nearly all of you students have something that is going to hamper you as long as you live. Most people go through life weighted down with something that is perfectly curable. They don't even need grace to get rid of some faults. A little common sense would get rid of them. There are a great many faults that you

could cure by adjusting your mental processes. You
don't even need to pray about them. *God never uses
the supernatural when the natural will work.* God won't
give you Divine power when your human mind can
accomplish the results. If I were you I would make
up my mind to get rid of my faults.

Your Manager, the Lord Jesus Christ, has put you
on a race track. He has fixed it all up for you. Get
rid of your besetting sin. You have a besetting sin.
When I say "besetting sin," everybody in this house
thinks of some weakness in his own life. You could
say "besetting sin" to me and I would think of my
weakness. I'll venture the assertion, I may be wrong
but I'll venture the assertion, that when I say "besetting sin" you think of yours. Some of you have a
temper. Some of you are selfish. Some of you are
bitter. Some of you are rebellious. God says that if
you are going to win the race you must get rid of the
sin that so easily besets you. You have a weak place.
There is a point in your character where Satan makes
an attack. The Allied Army in Italy is trying to find
a weak place to break through. The devil is trying to
find a point in your armor that he can penetrate. That
is what he is working for. I knew a preacher one time
who fell. A man said, "I am not surprised that he fell.
I saw him years ago cheat on examination in college."

You are to lay aside your besetting sin. Then you
are to do something else. You are to "run the race that
is set before you." "Run the race." Is that what the
Scripture says? What does it say? It says, "Let us
run with *patience*." I am the one who is being talked
to now. I want what I want and I want it now. I
despise a slow, dragging movement. I love a violin,

But this tuning the thing at the last minute never did appeal to me. In an evangelistic service the other night a girl was going to play the violin. She came out when I was already ten minutes late in starting the sermon. She got her violin and went ting, ting, ting, ting, ting, ting at the piano—ting, ting, ting, ting-ting, ting-ting! I thought I would almost die! Back in the old days when we had a violin on the vesper program here at the college the violinist would come out on the platform and go ting, ting, ting. One day I said, "Bob, you get a piano and put it behind the curtain and let them come out fiddling!"

Nobody but the Lord knows how much I have suffered from some things. I heard a man make an announcement the other day. I could have made the announcement, preached a sermon, called penitents, and pronounced the benediction while he was telling the people we would have another service the next day. Impatient! Impatient! How hard it has always been for me to stay with a thing. I want the results now. I have lived that kind of life. But there are results you can't get in a moment.

You can't win life's race in a moment. You can't build a character in a moment. You can be saved in a moment, but if you build a character that will stand the test of years and the storms of life you must give that character attention. You will never win in life unless you run with patience the race that is set before you. We have students who come here to school. They have high hopes and aspirations. They want to do something. They want to go places. But they stay here a few weeks and then get out of moral wind.

I can't help admiring the British. To think how they have held on! I admire the patience of the British. I admire the way the Russians have stuck it out. I know some people who never quit. They just hold on and hold on and hold on!

We have a great crowd of witnesses; the grandstand is full. We are on the race track. The Lord put us there! His strength is sufficient. He, figuratively speaking, calls us to one side and says, "I want to talk to you before you start. There are many people here today. Enoch is looking down on you. Abraham is looking down on you. Moses sees you. Heavenly hosts surround you. They are applauding you. They are hoping you will win! They know what you are up against; they had to run a race. They had their burdens, too; they were human as you are. But they won; and you can win, too! I will tell you how you can win. First, get rid of your weight. Whatever your weight is, get rid of it. Drop it."

Get rid of your besetting sin. Don't compromise with it. Don't play with it. Don't fool with it. If your eye offends you, pluck it out. Pull it out. It is not easy to pull out an eye, but pull it out! You had better have only one eye, and let that one be a good one. If your right hand is in your way, cut it off. It will hurt, but cut it off. Get rid of it right now! Remember Jesus will be with you in the race, and when you get out at the end of the track, He will be there and will have a crown for you. He will have it in His hand—His nail-pierced hand.

Young people, lay aside your sins and your faults, and be patient. You will get tired. It is a long track. This isn't just a little short road. It is a long one. It

is all through life. It may be many years. The road
is going to be rough. Be patient. Don't give up.
Jesus is the Author and the Finisher of your faith. *Run
with patience the race that is set before you!* God will
help you!

Prayer: "Our Heavenly Father, we pray Thee for a
Divine anointing and the infilling of the Holy Spirit
and the consecration we need. We pray for the will
power we need and the character we need. Help us to
go through with Thee. Lord, every one here has something he would be better off without, something that
handicaps him in the race. Help him to get rid of it.
Help us to help each other get rid of the things that
hinder.

"Now, we ask Thee to take care of this college.
Go with me as I go to Denver. Pour out the Holy
Spirit there. Be with Bob and the quartet in their
meetings in Buffalo. Be with these prayer captains in
the college. Lord, help these young people here to live
lives of prayer. Be with the faculty in their prayer
life. Bless those who have executive responsibility. Be
with the Director of Religious Activities and his assist-
ants, and be with the Dean. Be with the Business
Manager. Help him to be able to get food for us. Take
care of the coal situation. Lord, Thou hast been wonderfully good to us. Help us to get more coal; we don't
want the people here to be cold. Help us! Do something for us. Thou art for this college. We believe
Thou art for it. Help us to stay in condition where
Thou canst keep on being for us. We thank Thee we
have the money to pay for groceries. We thank Thee
for the money. We thank Thee that we can pay the
teachers their salaries, that we can pay them what we

promised them and sometimes more than we promised them. We thank Thee for Thy wonderful love and mercy and grace. Thou hast been so good to us. We wonder at it because there is nothing good about us. We are poor, miserable, blundering sinners. We don't deserve anything from Thee. Some of us don't deserve to be here. Maybe there is somebody who in his heart knows he isn't fit to be here. If there is such an one here, help him to get right. Keep this school right, Lord! Help us to keep faithful to God and true to His purpose. Don't let any of these buildings burn down. Thou hast been so good about that. Keep the students from accident and harm and danger. Nobody ever had a serious, permanent injury from an accident in this school. How wonderfully good Thou hast been to us through the years! We give Thee all the glory! We don't give it to anybody else. We couldn't have done it ourselves. *We give Thee all the glory and all the praise!* Now keep us while we are absent one from the other. Help every student here to feel his individual responsibility to the limit of his ability and the limit of his influence to preserve the spiritual atmosphere and standards of this school. *Lord, don't let us waver, don't ever let us waver!* For Jesus' sake we pray. Amen."

First Love Lost

"Unto the angel of the church of Ephesus write; These things saith He that holdeth the seven stars in His right hand, who walketh in the midst of the seven golden candlesticks;

"I know thy works, and thy labour, and thy patience, and how thou canst not bear them which are evil: and thou hast tried them which say they are apostles, and are not, and hast found them liars:

"And hast borne, and hast patience, and for My name's sake hast laboured, and hast not fainted.

"Nevertheless I have somewhat against thee, because thou hast left thy first love.

"Remember therefore from whence thou art fallen, and repent, and do the first works; or else I will come unto thee quickly, and will remove thy candlestick out of his place, except thou repent."

I HAVE read the first 5 verses of the 2nd chapter of the book of Revelation. I want you to stop for just a moment and think about who is speaking in these verses. The value of a statement is measured, to a great extent, by the one who makes the statement. For instance, if I made a statement about architecture, it would not have much value, because I do not know much about architecture. If I should say something about science, it wouldn't mean very much, because I don't know much about science. You always judge the weight of a statement by the man who made it. A single word from President Roosevelt who is now in the

Mediterranean war zone would make the first page of every paper in America.

The Lord Jesus Christ is speaking to the church at Ephesus. He is telling this church what He knows about them. God always knows about people. He knows about you. You can't palm a sham life off on Him. He sees every thought that walks across your brain. He knows every desire in your heart. He sees all the Bob Jones College students at one time. He sees earth's teeming millions at one time. Yet He sees every individual in the group here at Bob Jones College, and every individual in the teeming millions of the earth.

God Himself speaks. He is talking to the church at Ephesus. I want you to notice what He says about this church. When I read these words last night in my office and then again this morning, I said to myself, "I never saw a church that seemed to be in such fine condition." Notice what God says about it: "I know thy works." Their works were not the efforts they had made, but the achievements they had accomplished *through* the efforts they had made. God says in effect, "I know what you have done. I know your achievements, and I know how you have labored to produce them." He knew how much they had sweated, how much they had struggled, how much they had toiled. We don't always know, but God knows. God knows how much the mother toils to bring a baby up. God knows how much a father sweats at home to send the son or daughter to college. God knows the labor that produces the works. God says about this church, "I know all about you. I know what you have done. I know your achievements. I know your labor, and I know your patience." They were *patient* while they were laboring to produce their works. It is hard to be patient, isn't it? You get impatient, don't you?

You do here at school, some of you. If you want to overcome your impatience, get a goal fixed in your life and then look toward that goal. You can struggle through a great many things if you have your eye on the right goal.

I read in the Bible about a man who worked seven years so he could marry a girl. At the end of the seven years the old father-in-law seems to have tricked him a little, and he started in for seven years longer. He kept struggling for fourteen years because he wanted a woman he loved. Some of you can't wait six months. Some of you don't want to wait until you get out of college. You want to break off in the middle of school. But here is a man who, because he loved a woman, worked through fourteen years of struggle in order to marry her. And the years passed quickly.

This church at Ephesus had patience. God says something else about it, too. He says the members had convictions—"I know how thou canst not bear them which are evil." I want you to notice this. These people could put up with evil inside their organization. He is not saying to them here, "You wouldn't bear evil outside." He is saying that they wouldn't bear evil inside. A great many people can stand evil inside better than they can outside. But these people couldn't; they had convictions. They said, "If you are going to be in the church you ought to be somebody, you ought to be sincere and genuine and straight. You ought not to be a hypocrite and a liar and claim to be an apostle when you are not." They were intolerant of the man inside who wasn't right. They had convictions. You know what you young people need? You need convictions! In the old days everything was black or white. Now the color is dull gray.

We used to say, "This is right, and this is wrong." Now we say, "I don't know whether this is right or whether it is wrong." We need a line of demarcation between that which is right and that which is wrong. We have had students come to Bob Jones College and cover up the sins of other students and shield other students who were trying to scuttle the college ship as it sailed the tempestuous sea of our modern world. That is wrong. The members of the church at Ephesus were intolerant of evil inside. They said, "We are not going to have anybody in here 'messing up' our church. We are not going to have anybody who is a hypocrite or a liar or a humbug. We are not going to have a crook in this church." And God is commending these people because they had convictions. He says, "You have high standards."

They not only had convictions but they also had the *courage* of their convictions. What did they do? They tried these fellows, found them to be liars, and put them out. A great many people have convictions without courage. They say, "I know what is wrong. I know we shouldn't do that. I know that isn't right." But what do they do about it? Conviction without courage does not amount to much. Not only do we in this country need to know what is right and what is wrong, but we also need the courage to stand for that which is right and to stand against that which is wrong. We need the courage of our convictions. The average young person goes with the crowd, no matter which way the crowd goes. They have no convictions, no courage. They say, "Well, I just hate to take a stand." Listen! If you don't learn to stand for something, you'll never amount to anything!

I remember back in the old days when I lived in a certain southern city the good people wanted a campaign to clean up the city. The city was getting in a terrible condition. There was open immorality and sin. The ministers and a few other people said, "We must do something about it." And they asked me to head a campaign to clean up the city. I went to a prominent Baptist deacon and said to him, "You are a Christian, a business-man, and I want you to make a little speech at the mass meeting, telling what you think about the moral conditions in our city." He said, "I am in business; I can't express myself."

I went to see a prominent Methodist steward and said to him, "You have said 'Amen' in my evangelistic meetings many times. I am going to give you a chance to say 'Amen' at a big mass meeting. It may cost you something, but I will give you a chance to say it so you can be heard." "Oh," he said, "Brother Bob, you know I am with you—I am for you; but I can't express myself. It would ruin my business."

I then went to see a Presbyterian elder. I thought he was foreordained to help me! I said, "I want you to take a little time next Sunday to stand on the platform and tell the people something." "Oh," he said, "Listen, Brother Bob, you know me. I have always been for you—I am always for the thing that is right; but I can't express myself."

There was a Baptist deacon, a Methodist steward, and a Presbyterian elder, all supposed to be on God's side, all supposed to be standing for what was right; but when an issue arose they wouldn't, because they feared they would lose some money, *express* themselves. They ought to have been *expressed out of their churches.*

What we need in this country is a group of Christians with manhood and womanhood. We need young Christians who not only have convictions but who also have the courage to express those convictions! Christians ought to be able to say, "This is wrong. This is right. Let us do right and not do wrong." Those Christians at Ephesus had convictions and they also had the courage to carry out their convictions.

They had something else. They had the spirit of *endurance.* A great many people labor without having the spirit of endurance. Let us see if I can make it plain and simple. A man who *bears* things as a Christian, is a man who labors under difficulty. Endurance is the ability to do your work under difficulty. You must learn to do God's work under the difficulties of a terrible age. How easily some of us get out of wind! Some of you started out the first of the year to run a race for God. But the first thing you knew your tongue was hanging out. You were panting like a tired dog. Your wind was all gone. A horse I used to drive could travel the first mile as well as anybody's horse. But he didn't have the wind to keep going. Many Christians do not have endurance. When the labor becomes difficult and the opposition great, they get out of moral wind. But these Christians at Ephesus had borne things.

Let us go ahead. They had patience while they were bearing things. Paul did his work under great difficulty. Did you ever stop to think how he had to write some of those Epistles? Some of you don't like to get your lessons at night under a beautiful electric light in a steam-heated building. The Apostle had to sit in a dungeon. He would say, "Take this down for me." Then when he signed one of his Epistles he would say, "See what large handwriting I had to use; my eyes are bad, so excuse my writing." He worked under difficulty. You must learn to work under difficulty. God Almighty has put you in a difficult world. The devil is going to add to your difficulties. Day by day you must learn to do your job under difficulty!

God said something else about the people in this church at Ephesus. He said, "You went ahead and did all this labor and you bore up under it with patience. Not only that, you did it *for My name's sake.*" It looks to me as if these people were on a high plane. They were doing all these wonderful things: enduring, being patient, standing for the right, casting out hypocrites and liars; and they were doing them in the name of Jesus. I salute the church at Ephesus!

But God says, "I have something against you. You don't love Me as you used to." Do you know what Jesus Christ wants? *He wants your love.* He loved you so much that He died for you, and He wants you to love Him.

Robert E. Lee said, "Duty is the noblest word in the English language." He was right. But it is a cold word. There isn't much fire in it. It is one thing for a mother to lean over the bed of a sick child night after night. It is another thing for a nurse to do it. The nurse may be more efficient. She may be more capable. She may know how to take the baby's temperature and how to put the baby in cold packs when necessary; but there is a lack in the touch somehow. The nurse does her duty. But the baby will look up beyond the nurse and cry for its mother. The mother will wait on the baby and wait on the baby, and never get tired. She has the fire of a mother's love burning in her bosom.

I may be talking to some student in Bob Jones College at this very chapel hour who knows the love of God has died down in his heart. I could name a student who came to this school a radiant, enthusiastic, fervent, sweet Christian—a wonderful Christian! She is still a Christian, but she has settled down to the grind of a daily routine of school work—and having dates. I have observed this year that the love fire she used to have for her Lord has gone down. Once I could speak the name of Jesus in her ear and a light would come into her eyes. You can now whisper the name of a boy in her ear and a light comes in her eye. You can talk about Jesus and it doesn't move her. There is nothing against the girl. She is a good student. She attends to her duties all right. She keeps the rules. She obeys the law. She works. She tugs and toils. But the old fire of her first love for her Lord has gone down in her heart! I have seen the same thing many times.

That was what was the matter with these people in the church at Ephesus. They had convictions. They had a creed. They stood for something—they cast out the hypocrites and the liars and said, "We are going to keep this thing clean. This is the best church in this country and we are going to keep it that way." But God said, "You have lost the fervent, sweet love you used to have."

Have I got your number? Do you love Jesus as you used to love Him? Does your soul get all stirred when somebody sings, "What a Friend we have in Jesus all our sins and griefs to bear"? Have you lost your first love? Say, listen! a great many of you may have lost some of the other things that this Ephesian church had. You are not even on the plane they were on, and you have lost your first love, too.

Love is the highest mountain in God's range of mountains. That is God's Pike's Peak. And you fell off. Oh, you may be on some other mountains, but not on the highest mountain—not the mountain that sticks its head through the sky. You fell off that mountain. You fell on the mountain of duty or the mountain of service; but you are off the mountain of love. The fire of love went out, or cooled down.

Now you take Jesus for granted. One time you fell in love with Jesus. You said, "Jesus, You can have everything I have." Jesus took you and put His arms of love about you and you started life together. Then you got to where you took Him for granted. That is the way some men treat their wives. A man falls in love with a girl. She is sweet, lovely, beautiful, kind. He brings her flowers. If she sends him a flower he presses it and keeps it. If he has one of her tiny little handkerchiefs, he treasures it because it speaks to him of her. After awhile they are married. The routine of life comes on. He is true to her all right. He works for her, pays the doctor's bill, buys the groceries. But he settles down to the grinding routine and all the romance goes out.

That is the way you treated Jesus. You haven't gone back on Him. You just don't love Him as you used to. He is a sort of meal ticket. You ask Him to take care

of you, and you think He is all right; but you just don't
love Him very much.

When you fell in love with a girl, you thought that
girl incorporated in her personality your ideal. You
loved her because you thought she had in her the thing
you wanted in a woman. Maybe you found later that
you were mistaken. But you can't say anything like
that about Jesus. He has not changed. He is everything you thought He was—He is more than you
thought He was! He is the Son of God. He is the
compassionate, tender, wonderful, loving Saviour! He
watches over you and keeps you and preserves you.
He pumps the air into your lungs every day so you
can breathe. He stays awake and watches over you
while you sleep at night. He walks across the campus
with you and protects you from harm and danger. He
is everything you thought He was, and more. But you
don't love Him as you once did. You know I am telling
you the truth. You have lost your first love. There are
students in this college listening to me this morning
over whom Jesus Christ leans now and says, "Why
don't you love Me? Oh, you witness for Me all right.
You read your Bible, and you pray, and you tell everybody that I am all right. But I want you to love Me."

Did you ever hear a cracked bell ring in the belfry
of a church? There is no golden tone there. It sounds
like brass—a tinkling cymbal. Another bell can ring
which is no louder, maybe; but there is a golden tone
there. That is what love is. It gives the golden tone
to the bell when it is rung. If you don't have it, you
can make noise but not music. You can do good deeds,
but something is lacking. You can witness for Christ,
but it is the kind of testimony that doesn't carry much

weight. You can say, "I love Him," but people say, "She didn't have the right tone of voice."

Somebody asks, "Do you love me?" You answer, "Uh-huh." That person says, "You don't say it as if you mean it." That is the way you talk about Jesus. You don't say it as if you mean it. And the reason you say it that way is because you have lost your first love. You use the same language. You express yourself in the same way. But you somehow just can't say it right. It is like somebody singing "The Messiah" without having the Messiah in her heart. The greatest voice in the world doesn't sound exactly right unless the song is in the heart before it comes by way of the vocal chords through the mouth. You can't write beautiful poetry unless it comes from your heart. All beautiful poetry, all the hymns of praise, all the songs we sing about Jesus, must come up through the heart of Christian experience, if they move people.

But you can get the love back. God says, "I'll tell you how to get it back if you want it. Do the first works again—repent, and do the first works."

A man loved a beautiful girl when he and she were young. Later they were married. He was busy with the routine of business life, and she was busy with the routine of the home. The years passed. The fingers of Time pinched some wrinkles in his face and some wrinkles in hers, too. The frost of winter fell on her head and most of his hair had been pulled out by the hands of passing years. One day they were sitting by the fireside. He looked over at her and wondered if she could really be the girl he used to know. He slipped off alone into another room and found a picture of them which they had made when they were on their honeymoon. He looked in a mirror at himself and said, "I have grown old, too." And he went back and worshipped again at the shrine of the youthful days. The old fire of romantic love broke out in his heart. Then he went to her and said, "You are so beautiful! I love that white hair. I wish it would just stay white like that forever and forever!"

One time you fell in love with Jesus. He was beautiful then. And He hasn't grown old as we grow old. He is "the same yesterday, and today, and for ever"! You have just got used to being with Him, that is all. You have taken Him for granted. Why don't you go back and say, "One time He saved me. I was a poor, miserable, lost sinner on my way to Hell. In mercy He reached down, picked me up and saved me. He took me out of my sin and made me all I am." Remember what He has done for you. Do your first works over. And then you will fall in love with Him anew.

"I have somewhat against thee." The Lord said to the church at Ephesus, "You are doing some good all right. You are hard workers. You have convictions. You are patient. You have endurance. You have many wonderful things about you. But I want you to love Me." Remember, young people, Jesus Christ would rather have your love than your service. Does He have your love?

Let us all stand and sing, "Oh, how I love Jesus." If you love Him, I want you to sing. If you don't love Him, don't sing. I am not asking you to sing this song just to make music. Before we sing it, let us have a moment of prayer.

Prayer: "O Lord, Thou knowest our hearts. We remember how Simon Peter said, 'Thou knowest that I love Thee.' And we believe in our hearts we do love Thee. We have just been neglectful of telling Thee about it sometimes. We have been so neglectful. We bring Thee today a bouquet of praise and we bring Thee a Christmas present of our own heart's affection. We give Thee our bodies for service. This is a love gift. If we have any talent that we have held back from Thee we would give that talent to Thee today—whatever it is. Help us to really love Thee; and now may we be able to sing from our hearts, "Oh, how I love Jesus.""

The student body sing:

> "Oh, how I love Jesus!
> Oh, how I love Jesus!
> Oh, how I love Jesus!
> Because He first loved me!"

Dr. Jones: "Our Heavenly Father, help us to always love Thee and be true to Thee in the midst of the terrible conditions of our modern world. We pray in Thy name. Amen."

Is God Pleased?

I AM reading from the 10th chapter of I Corinthians, beginning with the 1st verse:

"Moreover, brethren, I would not that you should be ignorant, how that all our fathers were under the cloud, and all passed through the sea; and were all baptized unto Moses in the cloud and in the sea; and did all eat the same spiritual meat; and did all drink the same spiritual drink; for they drank of that spiritual Rock that followed them; and that Rock was Christ." In other words, they all had the same advantages. They had access to the same testimony. They had contact with the same spiritual power. "But with many of them God was not well pleased."

I wonder how He feels about you this morning! I wonder if He is pleased with the record you have made in the four months you have been in Bob Jones College. You have had access to the testimony. There has been more prayer in Bob Jones College these four months than ever went up from the college in any other nine months of its history. There has been more effort —sincere, "honest-to-goodness" effort—made this year to put on the proper spiritual pressure than we have ever made in the history of the institution. Personally, I have given more concentrated thought to the spiritual welfare of this school than I have ever done in any other year. I have sat in my office by the hour this past summer and prayed and planned. We opened the school year with a revival. Some of you have been saved since you came here. There has been spiritual emphasis in every department. The power of God has been manifest in a wonderful way. You have all had access to all the spiritual training and blessing.

"But with many of them God was not well pleased; for they were overthrown in the wilderness." God always shows it when He isn't satisfied. Don't you ever forget that! If God Almighty isn't satisfied with you, He will demonstrate His dissatisfaction. He doesn't cover up His disapproval. I don't care who you are, if God is disapproving your life, He will let you know about it some way or other, that is, if you have enough spiritual sense to understand God. Many people have trouble in this world because they don't treat God right. God won't let Bob Jones College boys and girls get away with anything. I have seen them try it. He won't let them do it!

"For they were overthrown in the wilderness. Now these things were our examples, to the intent we should not lust after evil things, as they also lusted." That is what some of you may have been doing. You have been here in this atmosphere, and you may have been lusting after evil things. You may have been wanting to get out from under the restraints—out where you would have the liberty and freedom of a wicked world and where you wouldn't have to march under orders. These people are an example to us.

"Neither be ye idolaters, as were some of them; as it is written, The people sat down to eat and drink, and rose up to play." That is the way they lived. That is the way the world is living now. They were interested in their appetites and pleasures and didn't want any restrictions about them.

"Neither let us commit fornication, as some of them committed, and fell in one day three and twenty thousand." God doesn't let folks get away with immorality. Certainly He does not let His own saved people get away with immorality. If you go away from Bob Jones College and this atmosphere of Christian culture to play the loose game of this sensual age, God Almighty will throw a thunderbolt of His wrath at you. He won't let you get away with it! Don't you dare think that you can play with God's justice and God's judgment and God's moral law!

"Neither let us tempt Christ, as some of them also tempted, and were destroyed of serpents." Don't you, because you are a Christian, presume upon the goodness and mercy of God.

"Neither murmur ye." They murmered. They murmured about the restraints they were under. I am reading current literature to you this morning. Human nature still resents the restraints of decency. The children of Israel said, "We don't like it this way. It is too strict and too straight. We don't want to march under orders. We don't like it when somebody tells us what to do." Men still murmur when they are restrained. God said the children of Israel would be destroyed by the destroyer. And the destroyer did destroy them.

"Now all these things happened unto them for ensamples." Why did all these things happen to them? So *we* wouldn't act the fool. They "got it in the neck" so we could save our necks. I am talking the plain language of everyday living. They got hit on the nose so you wouldn't get your nose broken. "Now all these things happened unto them for ensamples; and they are written for our admonition." God says, "I am putting them in the Book. I am letting you know what happened to these people—these people who didn't like the rules, who didn't like the restraint, who wanted freedom and liberty and wanted to throw off the yoke because they did not wish to pull the load of obedience." They didn't get away with it. Remember God made a record of the fact for our admonition "upon whom the ends of the world are come."

"Now, listen! "Wherefore (in view of this record, this tragic record, this record of disobedience, this record of rebellion, this record of God's judgment against them for their sins) let him that thinketh he standeth take heed lest he fall." If you don't watch your step during these holidays you may be wringing your hands and saying, "O God, why did I do it!" Watch your step! When you walk off this campus, when you walk out from under the regulations that govern conduct in this institution and go home for the holidays, our responsibility, beyond our obligation to pray for you, ends.

We are under obligation to God and to you while you are here to hedge you about, to protect you, to shield you as far as possible, and to teach you the Christian philosophy of life. We are under obligation to help you in every way we can help you, to stimulate you spiritually, to warn you of dangers and put about you the best protecting power that it is possible for us to find in both finite and infinite resources. We have done our best. If when you step off this campus you go back on God, grieve the Holy Spirit, smear your

Christian testimony, and get in trouble, your blood will be on yourself, not on us.

Let us read further. God wants to encourage you. He wants you to know that all these people to whom He refers had temptations. Some yielded to the temptations. They were bitten by serpents and perished in the wilderness. But they didn't have to yield to temptation. And *you* don't have to yield.

"There hath no temptation taken you but such as is common to man." The word "common" means something shared by one person with somebody else. You and the friend who is a friend to you are mutual friends. A common friend is a man who is a friend to you and a friend to me, a person whose friendship we both share. Many people get these words mixed up. They say, "He is our mutual friend." He is your common friend if he is your friend and the other person's friend, too.

"There hath no temptation taken you but such as is common to man." Temptation is old. The tragedy of the fall is old. The fact that folks can't do wrong and get away with it is old. There hath no temptation taken you but such as is common to man: but God (God who never let anybody down!) is faithful, who will not suffer you to be tempted above that ye are able." God never put anything on any man he could not stand. God never permitted any human being to be tempted beyond his ability to win. No temptation ever came to any man in all the world but that by the power of God that man could have won!

"There hath no temptation taken you but such as is common to man; but God is faithful, who will not suffer you to be tempted above that ye are able; *but*

will with the temptation also make a way to escape."
When temptation sets the house on fire, there is a fire
escape! You do not have to fall. God will give you
victory if you really want it.

God will never drop from the sky a supernatural
fire escape if a natural fire escape is sufficient. Do you
know one of the best ways of escape you have when
you are tempted? You have two legs, haven't you?
Those legs were given to you by the same God who gave
His Son to die for you. If you deliberately stick yourself under the nose of temptation, God Almighty will
let the devil get you; and he ought to have you! You
dirty compromiser, he ought to have you! God says,
"Flee youthful lusts." Take no chance. Use your legs;
run, run! Now, if you didn't have any legs, if you
couldn't run, God would hedge you about with a new
and supernatural protection. God would say, "Here is
a crutch. Use it." But you have two good legs. You
don't have to have a crutch. If you get back with that
"old gang" during the holidays, the "old gang" you
used to run with; if you get off on some joy-ride and
breathe that old cigarette smoke you used to breathe;
if you put yourself back with that old crowd that you
used to go to parties with before you came to Bob
Jones College, the devil is going to get you. Remember
I warned you. Watch your step! Don't you come back
with the smell of hell on you, I don't care who you are!

I pray that God Almighty will take care of you girls
and boys; you are not any common herd. God save our
girls from the wicked influence of the sensual, wicked
age in which we live! You girls all profess to be
Christians. Remember your body is the temple of the
Holy Ghost. You boys, preserve your Christian in-

tegrity. Never mind what other young men do. Remember God said, "Have no confidence in the flesh." Stay away from that "old gang." Avoid the very appearance of evil—the very *appearance* of it!

I told you young people the other day that you might get in a close place sometime. There may be walls on every side of you. You may be completely surrounded. It may be that you can't run away. So what are you going to do? Just look up and trust God and He will come down through the roof into the building with you. He will say, "I am not going to let the devil have this fellow." But if you can run away and won't run, God Almighty is not going to run down, pick you up in His arms, and run off with you. Use your legs! Don't be lazy spiritually.

Somebody is probably leaving here today who will never get back. We have never had Christmas holidays, as far as I know, except once or twice, when everybody got back. There is usually somebody who doesn't have enough character to come back and finish the semester and take chances on passing his work. Nearly every Christmas somebody goes home who is not able to get back—something happens that makes it so he can't get back. I may be talking to some of you for the last time. I don't know the future, but I know God, and I know human nature; and I am telling you something today that I want you to remember as long as you live: *You can't do wrong and get away with it!*

Not even a Christian can do wrong and get away with it. You can't beat the game of sin! You just can't do it. God won't let you do it. Remember that! But you don't have to fall. No temptation will ever come to you that some other saint hasn't some time had. There is nothing new in satanic strategy. He has no secret weapon. He has used already on the human race every weapon he ever invented in his satanic brain and forged in his shop of hellish hatred against God and man.

Remember if you deliberately put yourself in the way of temptation you are not getting ready to yield; *you have already yielded!* You have already fallen because God told you to *avoid the appearance of evil.* When you unnecessarily expose yourself, you disobey God. To disobey God is to fall.

When you walk out of this building and off this campus you are going to walk into the coldest air you have ever felt. You don't know how this world has changed in the last four months. It isn't the same world it was four months ago. Leaving this Christian center is like walking out of a steam-heated building into zero weather without any clothes to keep you warm. I am warning you. You don't have to have spiritual pneumonia. You don't have to have moral "flu." You can breathe God's air, hold your shoulders up, put your chest out, pull your stomach in, stick your chin out, and look to God. He will give you victory. You can shake your fist in the face of the devil and spit in hell and come back decent! I expect you to come back decent. God wants you to come back decent. So do it.

Prayer: "Our heavenly Father, we thank Thee for Thy wonderful love and blessing. We thank Thee for Thy keeping power and grace. There are some students here this morning who have been saved this fall. Others have found God's will for their lives. Some have learned to really pray. Some have learned how to live in fellowship with Thee. Some have found victory in the Lord

Jesus Christ. Thou hast been so good to us. Thou hast blessed this college that tells the whole world we believe the Bible from cover to cover. Now Christmas has come. Some of us are going to stay here. Some of us are leaving for home for a little while. Some are going home on buses and trains and some in cars of their own. They are going to have congested traffic. Some are going to have a hard time traveling but a wonderful opportunity for Christian testimony. Help them to be faithful! Give us who are here rest of body, of nerves, of mind, and of heart. Bless us all together, those who go and those who stay. Keep us from falling. Thou wilt have to help us, for nobody else can. We are looking to Thee for victory in the name of Jesus Christ our Lord. Amen."

Now wait a minute. I want us to stand and sing before we leave, one stanza of "Blest be the tie that binds our hearts in Christian love." While we sing I want every student here this morning to go to some other student who has been a spiritual blessing to him this year and shake hands with him or her and say, "Thank you."

Hundreds of students moved from place to place in the building to thank other students for helping them spiritually. The entire hymn, "Blest Be the Tie That Binds," was sung, followed by two verses of "God Be With You Till We Meet Again." Then Dr. Jones said, "All right! Merry Christmas! Faithful Living! God be with you!"

Results of Riotous Living

"The younger son gathered all together, and took his journey into a far country, and there wasted his substance with riotous living" (Luke 15:13).

THE son is not the hero of the story of the prodigal son. There is a tendency on the part of human nature to make a sinner the hero. The sinner is never the hero.

Sometimes an evangelist advertises himself as a converted jailbird or as a converted gangster. I never like that kind of advertising. It is all right to advertise Gypsy Smith as a gypsy, because he is a gypsy. He was converted as a gypsy boy and was brought up in a gypsy tent. It is all right to speak of Billy Sunday as an ex-baseball player, for that was what he was. Being a gypsy is a legitimate business and being a baseball player is also legitimate business. It is all right to talk of Dwight L. Moody as having been a shoe drummer. That is what he was, and selling shoes is legitimate business. But I never like to see men advertise themselves as converted jailbirds or converted thieves or converted burglars or converted gangsters. I know human nature too well. There is a danger of our thinking of the gangster instead of the Saviour who can save the gangster.

I am always a little uneasy when a man with a bad past gives his life's story. It is possible to tell that kind of story for the glory of God, and it is sometimes so told. But it is often told in a spirit of boasting about the sin the man has committed. I don't like to see the sinner made the hero. The sinner is never a hero in any of God's "dramas." This prodigal son "played opposite" the father who was the hero in this drama.

Get the picture clearly: Jesus was preaching one of the straightest sermons ever preached. The Pharisees were listening to Him. They were watching Him because He was healing on the Sabbath. I can see the expressions of scorn and contempt on their faces. Jesus finished the 14th chapter of Luke by saying, "He that hath ears to hear, let him hear," and the publicans and sinners moved up close to Him. Jesus had been preaching to the Pharisees and the lawyers, the religious leaders of the day. He had not been defending publicans and harlots. He had been condemning the sin of men who were not interested in publicans and harlots.

There has never been one word uttered by Almighty God in defense of the sins that men commit. He never defends or condones sin. He pities the sinner. He didn't condone the sin of the woman whom the scribes and Pharisees were about to stone. He said, "If you are guiltless, throw a stone at her." He didn't condone her sin. He never does condone sin. And when you begin to condone sin you have reached the very gate of damnation.

When the publicans and sinners moved up close to Jesus He began to show them the Father's heart through the parables which He spoke. He began to show them that God loved them. The heroine of the first parable was the woman who looked for the coin. The coin was a mere incident. The hero in the second parable was the shepherd, not the sheep. The hero in the third parable was the father, not the son.

The prodigal son was a bad boy. Don't you try to make him a good boy. Don't you try to exalt him.

Don't you forget his sin. God doesn't want you to forget the sins that sinners commit. Sin is a terrible thing. It has terrible consequences, as I shall show before I finish the message this morning.

The prodigal son started downgrade. He manifested a restlessness because of the restraints of home. He didn't like to have his father tell him when to get up in the morning. He didn't like the refining, restraining presence of his mother. He chafed under his surroundings. That is always the first step on the road to degradation. That is the first step that Eve made in the Garden of Eden. She chafed under the restraints that surrounded her. The person who doesn't want to be restrained by an atmosphere of decency, whether he knows it or not, has started on the downward road. The fellow who doesn't want the restraint of culture wants the atmosphere of that which is common and cheap.

I can imagine the prodigal son possibly said to his older brother, "I am tired of this place. I don't like it. I want what is coming to me. Mother is a good woman. You are a hard worker. But I just don't like this place. I am not free." If he had been a modern boy he might have said, "I want an automobile so I can ride when I please. I want an automobile so I can park by the roadside on dark nights." He might also have said, "I like to take a glass of beer when I want it. You don't have any beer here. I want to gratify my appetite." Let me tell you something! If you are chafing under restraint, if your soul rises up today to push back restriction, you have taken the first step on the downward road.

This boy did something else. He overemphasized his personal rights. Don't misunderstand me. You have personal rights. You have a right to use your eyes. You ought to protect them. You ought to protect your hearing. There are certain property rights to which men are legitimately entitled and they should by legitimate procedure protect them as far as possible. There isn't anything in the Bible that denies us our personal rights. The Scripture says, "Look not every man on his own things, but every man *also* on the things of others." You are not to be indifferent to your things, but you are to remember that the other man has things, too. The prodigal son said, "I want my rights." He was entitled to certain things, but he overemphasized his rights.

The prodigal son did not want to enjoy his rights in the right way. He wanted to get what was coming to him and use it as he pleased. He said, "Give me my share of the living. You have things here I am entitled to. I want them." He went into a far country.

I know a girl who belongs to a good family and who has been in a Christian college for two or three years, but she doesn't like it because there are certain restraints thrown about her. She has always wanted her way. She wanted her way at home when she was a child. She has many good traits, some talents, and an average mind; but she just doesn't like to be restrained. She is going to a great university where she can do as she pleases. The story of the prodigal son is current literature. It is the thing that is on the pages of every American newspaper. It is not old stuff; it is up-to-date.

The prodigal son went away—away where he couldn't see the light in his mother's window, away where he couldn't see his old gray-headed father looking up the road, away where he couldn't come home at night with a dread that dad would still be awake, away where he couldn't hear his mother say, "Is that you, son? Your bed is ready. Good night, my boy." He wanted to get away from that mother's gentle voice. He wanted to get away from the familiar bark of the dog and the lowing of the cattle. He couldn't be comfortable there. He wanted to get away, and he went into a far country.

He wasted his substance. His substance really was not *his* substance. His own brother said to his father, "He hath devoured *thy* living." Somebody wrote a song entitled, "What Have We That We Have Not Received?" After all, your money isn't your money. Your health isn't your health. If there is a rose of health blooming in your cheek today, God planted the rose! If you have a strong right arm, God gave it to you. You say, "This is my right arm." Yes, it is; but God gave it to you. What have you done with your substance? Your talents were handed down by God Almighty over the battlements of Heaven. What have you done with them? Anything you have which is used for yourself and not for God is wasted substance.

The prodigal son "wasted his substance with riotous living." If he had written a check and given all he had to missions, the "society crowd" would have said, "What a fool!" But to the worldly, godless society crowd he was a "wise boy." He sacrificed his father's substance on the altar of his own lust.

In the next place—and I am sure of this—he was immoral. That is what his brother said about him, and his brother knew him pretty well. They had grown up together. They had played together. They may have said their prayers at night together. They had had their little fights. The older son may have heard his prodigal brother say a dirty word one day. He knew him, and he said to his father, "I am not coming to his feast. I am not going to sit down at the table—not with him! He wasted your hard-earned money with harlots."

It was all right for this brother to take his stand against his wasting the money on harlots. There wasn't anything wrong with the fact that the Pharisees and Sadducees looked on immorality with contempt. Really they had no right to justify the sins of publicans and the sins of harlots. Their sin was the sin of not loving harlots and publicans as God loved them. The sin of this older brother was that he didn't understand how a father feels when a boy repents. Don't be too hard on this elder brother.

I have heard many people ask, "How can God Almighty save him?" when some modern prodigal has come forward to take Christ as Saviour in an evangelistic service. This morning I had a letter from a sixteen-year-old boy who said, "I have been cuffed around all my life. My mother was sick and my daddy left her when I was a little baby. Mother put me in first one boarding-place and then in another and in first one school and then in another. I have had a hard time. I used to be mad with everybody. But a year ago I met Jesus. He fixed me up. I have been called to preach and I want to come to Bob Jones College. I am just in high school. If you have a high school I want to start right away. If you don't have a high school in connection with Bob Jones College, please tell me of one I can attend so I can be a preacher." I said to myself, "What a mean daddy to leave his own boy to be cuffed around and kicked about!" I have been preaching for forty-five years and I found myself saying when I read the letter, "I wonder if that father really should be saved?" Did you ever ask yourself a question like that? Did you ever ask yourself whether or not God ought to save Hitler even if he should repent?

This older brother was a Pharisee, and he was used as an example of the Pharisees by Jesus. He didn't understand God's love, and that was the trouble with the Pharisees. They didn't understand that God loves the sinner.

The prodigal son was immoral. He was the immoral type. Listen! You will probably wind up immoral if you chafe under restraints! You will wind up immoral if you clamor for your rights and move away from the light in the window and the voice of God. Don't "brag" too much on the prodigal son and make a hero out of him. He was a bad boy. He was "ornery"; he was mean.

Now, let us look for a moment at the consequences of the sins he committed. No man ever sinned without evil consequences. You can't do it even if God forgives you, offers you a pardoning kiss and fatherly embrace, and puts on your finger a ring signifying His forgiveness.

When I waked up early this morning and began to think about this message, I thought of the influence of the prodigal son in that far country. I wondered if when he sat down at the banquet table in the father's house there wasn't some poor drunken fellow in that far-away country staggering home to curse a wife and hungry child because he had led him into drink. Perhaps that man did not drink at all before that time the prodigal son offered him a drink. He may have said, "I don't drink." The prodigal son may have said, "Oh, come on! Be a good sport and have a drink. I have plenty of money; I will pay for the drink!" The man took the drink. A sleeping appetite for a stimulant waked up in his blood and he said, "Give me another one and another one." While the prodigal son sat at the feast given him by a forgiving father there may have been back in the far country a drunkard with a ragged wife and a starving child.

I wondered if there wasn't some broken home back in that far country because of the prodigal's influence. Perhaps some man and his wife were getting along all right until one day the shadow of a man with a pocket full of money fell across the steps of their home. Now the home is broken up. The little girl of the home stays with her mama one week and her daddy the next week.

I wondered if while he was sitting in the home at the feast there wasn't some woman back in the far country hugging to her bosom a little baby that had no father. Oh, boys and girls, men and women, some of us are conscious that behind us somebody has suffered because we sinned. Some of us can't forget it. God is good. He blots out our sins and hides them forever behind His back, but there are always evil consequences that follow the sinner even when his sins are forgiven.

The prodigal son had been forgiven. He had had a pardoning kiss. He was at a banquet. He had music and dancing. But I wonder if that night while he was dancing he didn't say, "I have a little pain in my back which I brought home with me from the far country." I wonder if in the years that came afterwards he didn't look at a scar on a little baby boy's face and wonder if that little scar was a transmitted disease which he had brought back from the far country. I just wonder.

An old preacher wrote me some time ago and said, "I am an old man. I have been saved many years, but I am still suffering in my body from the sins of my youth." The prodigal son never had the same body he had before he left home. No sinner ever had the same body after he sinned.

I wonder about his mind, too. I wonder if that day in the home as his mother and father beamed on him with love and forgiveness his diseased brain didn't reach a long hand across the country to that far-away place and pull out some memory of dissipation and sin.

Then there was his conscience. I can imagine he said, "Dad is so nice to forgive me. He is wonderful to give me a feast. But even all these things torment my conscience. I went away one time. I walked out from the home to a far-away land. I sinned and now, even though I have been forgiven, my conscience disturbs me.

Sin always separates. The rich man in hell said, "Don't let my brothers come down here!" As children, these two boys—the older son and the younger son—had played together. They had sat and talked together. One day the younger brother said, "I am going away to a far country to live my own life. You can stay here with the Old Man if you want to, but not me! I want every thing that is mine even if we have to break up this estate. I am going to another land." The older brother no doubt said, "I wouldn't go if I were you, brother. I wouldn't go. It is a wonderful place here." "But," he said, "I am going." There was a breach between them.

That is not all. Did you ever stop to think how much sorrow he caused his mother and dad? Young people, listen to me. People tell you that love is blind.

Love isn't blind. Love just doesn't always tell what it sees. I imagine that many a night the boy's father would turn over in bed and sigh. The mother would say, "What is the matter, can't you sleep?" The husband would reply, "Oh, I am all right. I just am not sleepy." "Are you worried about anything?" "No, not especially. I have a lot of business on my mind and I am a little tired tonight anyhow," he would answer. Do you know what that father was thinking about? He didn't tell his wife, but he remembered times when the boy as a small child had shown certain evil tendencies. The old man had never forgotten. He just didn't tell what he remembered, not even to the boy's mother. Charity is one of the names for love. The Bible says, "Charity covers . . ." It does cover. Love sees, but it doesn't always tell what it sees.

Perhaps your mother saw something in you when you were a little child. She has never forgotten it. She may have sent you to Bob Jones College, praying and hoping that the thing she feared might never come to pass. Love always sees.

No doubt many a sleepless night the prodigal's mother tried to be still so she wouldn't disturb the father, and the father tried to be still so he wouldn't disturb the mother. But their hearts were breaking. Did you ever do anything to dad or mother like that because you didn't like restraint?

From the *human standpoint* we might say two or three good things about the prodigal son. We might say that he had vision. We might say that he was big-hearted. I think he probably was, though he was selfish even in his generosity. We might say that he did get a job when he got broke—and, by the way, he didn't get a nice job, either. If he were a Jew, feeding hogs was the worst thing he could have done.

But from the *divine point of view* we can say just one good thing about him. He said, "I will arise and go to my father, and will say unto him, Father, I have sinned against heaven, and before thee, and am no more worthy to be called thy son; make me as one of thy hired servants." He could have said, "They mistreated me, Dad." He could have said, "You brought me up strict, and when I got out there I just fell." He could have said, "Dad, I got off a little mentally." He could have said, "Dad, there was a famine in that country. People lost all they had." He didn't make excuses. He just said, "I don't deserve anything, but I should like to come in if you will let me. I don't ask you to give me my old place. I don't deserve that. Give me any kind of job you want to give me. All I want is just to be around here where I can see the light in the window. I should like to be here where I can hear the cattle low. I should like to be here, Dad, where I can see you go up the steps. I don't deserve to be here, but won't you let me hoe the garden? Won't you let me curry the horse? Dad, I'll do anything, just anything." That is the only good thing you can say about him. There are many good things you can say about his father, but that is all you can say about the son. Listen! one of the signs the prodigal was fit to be a son was the fact that he was willing to be a servant. No man is entitled to a feast of forgiveness and a banquet of pardoning mercy who thinks he deserves them. Those who know they don't deserve them are the only ones who will ever have them.

How Are We Saved?

BEFORE you leave for the Christmas holidays I want to bring you a message on the question: *"How Are We Saved?"* I have two reasons for bringing this message. First, I want every Christian here, and I hope all of you are Christians, to be able during the Christmas holidays to tell somebody what to do to be saved. I don't want you to have any question in your mind about what you should say.

In the second place, if there should happen to be some student here who isn't a Christian, I want that student to know exactly what he must do to be saved. I want to make it so clear that there can never be a question in any of your minds about it. I want to fix it, not only for today, but for all the future. I want you to be able to tell anybody any time, anywhere, how to be saved.

My text this morning is the 8th and 9th verses of the 2nd chapter of Ephesians: *"For by grace are ye saved through faith; and that not of yourselves; it is the gift of God; not of works, lest any man should boast."*

Suppose at the close of this chapel service you could walk up to this platform and tell me the thing you want most, and suppose I had the power to give you that thing. What would you ask for? Some one says, "I would ask you for money." No, you wouldn't. People think they want money until they get it, but when they get it they find that isn't what they want

209

at all. I have said many times to people all over
America that the things that make men happy, money
cannot buy. Money cannot buy the love of a wife.
It may buy a wife, but no woman's love was ever sold
in the markets of the world. Money cannot buy peace
of conscience. Money cannot buy the peace that comes
to your heart when your mother kisses you goodnight
and tucks you in bed. Money cannot buy the thrill
that comes to your heart when you hold in your arms
your own baby. *The things that make men happy,
money cannot buy.* So, it is not money that people
want. They may think it is, but it isn't.

It is not position that men want. Some people think,
"If I had a certain position, I would be happy." You
wouldn't. Position never brought happiness to anybody. Some of the happiest people I have ever met in
my life have been lowly, humble people, living in ob-
scurity. Some of the most miserable people I have
known held prominent and influential positions.

I will tell you this morning what you want. The
thing you want most is harmonious life. Men want
to live, and they want to live harmoniously. I do not
think any sane man ever committed suicide. Do not
misunderstand me. Sometimes men are responsible for
their insanity, for some insanity is due to sin and men
are responsible for their sins. But when a man commits
suicide he is insane. No normal man ever blew a hole
through his head. No normal man ever leaped off a
house to commit suicide. No normal man ever went
home, closed the doors, stopped all the cracks and holes,
and turned on the gas to end his life. Normal men want
to live. A drowning man will instinctively reach for
anything he can get, even a straw. If you should

jump in a river to commit suicide, you would instinctively reach for something as you went down to keep
you from drowning. A dying man will struggle for
one more breath, however great may be the agony of
breathing. God put in the heart of man a love for
life. You want to live, and you want to live harmoniously.

If I could write a book that would tell people how to
live to be a hundred years old I could sell everybody
here a copy. I know what you would do, because I
bought a book like that myself one time. It was twenty-
five years ago. I was just thirty-five years old. I was in
a book store in a Pennsylvania town where I was conducting an evangelistic campaign. I picked up a book
on a counter in a book store. It had great big letters
on the outside which said, "Do what I say to do and you
will live to be a hundred years old." I said to the
clerk, "What is this book worth? I want to buy it."
I didn't try to pull her down on the price. I paid what
she asked and walked out with the book under my
arm. I went back to the apartment where Mrs. Jones
and Bob, Jr., who was a little fellow then, and I were
living. I said, "Now, don't anybody disturb me. I am
going to do just what this book says to do. It says
that if I will do what it says I will live a hundred
years. That will give me sixty-five more years."

I opened the book. The subject of the first chapter
was *diet*. Books like that always start at the most
disagreeable point! It said, "Don't eat so-and-so." I
said, "Now, listen, that is the best eating any fellow
ever did eat. That is an old stand-by. That has been
a friend of mine through the years." But the book
said, "Don't eat it. Give it up." "All right. I'll give

it up." Then the book said, "Don't eat so-and-so, either." And in three or four paragraphs the author eliminated all I like—and I like nearly everything!

The next chapter told me *what to eat*. I never read of such a conglomerated mess of eating put together anywhere in the world! It said, "Eat so-and-so." I said, "It just can't be eaten, that's all!" "All right, if you will eat it, you will live to be a hundred years old." "All right then, pass the grub! I'll eat it!" I made up my mind to give up all I liked and to eat what I didn't like because I wanted to live to be a hundred.

The next chapter was on the subject of *exercise*. That is always brought up sooner or later. Now, you may not realize it, but I have done nearly all the physical stunts that are "do"-able. I went to a gymnasium for weeks and weeks and weeks. I have actually taken cold baths in the morning before breakfast. For two long, agonizing years I took them! Now, you talk about your idea of a hero. I have *my* idea of a hero! My idea of a hero is a fellow who on a winter's morning ..en the temperature is around zero gets out of a warm bed, goes into the bathroom, fills the tub with cold water, stands there and looks at it, and then deliberately gets into it! When a man goes to war he doesn't deserve much credit for fighting. He sort of has to fight—like the colored fellow who was in the last World War. He said he didn't have anything against the Kaiser, and Uncle Sam couldn't make him fight. A fellow said, "No, he can't make you fight, but he can take you to where the fighting is going on and then you can exercise your own judgment!"

But this cold bath heroism is deliberate, foreordained, predestinated heroism. You make up your mind to be a hero—or a fool! You go to bed at night with the thing all planned for the next morning. I lived two miserable years like that! Life didn't mean anything to me. I went to bed at night knowing what was ahead of me the next morning! People told me if I would keep it up long enough I would get to where I wouldn't mind it, but the last one I took—I mean the last cold one!—was the coldest one I ever took. I was in a town in Illinois. It was twenty below zero. I got up that morning with the wind sounding a wailing, sympathetic, pitying note around the house. It was saying, "You poor fellow!" And I wept with the wind! I went into the bathroom and filled the tub. I studied about it a little while. I backed off and took a running start and I got in—for the last time! I haven't had one—I mean a cold one—since!

I have done everything to live. I went to a man years ago in Lynchburg, Virginia, who was supposed to have been the world's strong man at the World's Fair in Chicago. He was seventy-two years old and without a gray hair in his head. That man could lift, he said, hundreds of pounds. He had his own system of exercise. I said, "Now, Doctor, I want you to give me your system of exercise. I want to take a little time out every day and build a good body." He said to me, "I have been hearing you preach and observing your actions on the platform. You have unconsciously incorporated in your delivery, every lesson I ever gave in physical training. Just keep preaching and don't worry."

Well, the chapter on exercise in that famous book said, "When you wake up in the morning throw your cover back. Lift your right leg and say, 'Good morning.' Then lift your left leg and say, 'How do you do?' Then let your face and your feet meet and talk to each other for a few minutes. After they have had their little visit lift your right foot and then your left foot, your right hand and then your left hand"—early in the morning when you can't even lift your eyelids!

But what appealed to me was that that man knew how to write a title to a book. When he entitled the book "How To Live To Be A Hundred Years Old," he was appealing to that instinctive something in the soul of man that makes him want to live. Why, if I could add ten years to the average length of human life I would immortalize my name.

But one time about two thousand years ago there walked on this earth a Person who said He could make men live *forever*. He said, "I can give you *eternal life*. I can make you live as long as God, My Father, lives. I can make you live when suns go out and worlds are blotted out. I can make you live on and on and on! I can give you *eternal life*." Now, wait a minute! What a startling promise! We can increase the average of human life but a few years; and here is a lowly Galilean who says, "I can make you live forever."

If a man promised me something I would ask him two questions—I might not ask him aloud, but I would ask him in my mind: First, *can* you do what you say you will do? Second, *will* you do what you say you will do?

Now, when Jesus Christ promises me eternal life I am going to ask two questions: First, can He deliver? Can He do what He says He will do? Has He got the goods? Second, will He keep His word? Will He do it?" What do you think about Jesus Christ and His

ability to do what He said He would do? He was
always careful about what He said. He never exagger-
ated. He never promised anything He didn't do.

I told you last Sunday that Jesus Christ said He was
going to do four things. He has done two of them.
He is doing the third. He is going to do the fourth.
He said *He was going to die.* He said *He was going
to rise from the dead.* He said *He was going to build
His church.* And He said *He was coming again.* He
was never late at any time. He never promised a
thing He didn't do. He never said, "I'll be there," without being there. He keeps His Word. And He is able
to do it. He is the only person on earth who ever lived
who didn't have to say, "I'll be there," with a reserva-
tion in his mind. You say you are going home for
Christmas. You *think* you are going. You may or you
may not go. The bus may break down. The train
may be wrecked. You may die. You may not get on a
car. You *think* you are going. Jesus Christ, as I said
the other day, never said, "I think."

Look what He did! Nobody could stay dead around
Him. If a funeral procession passed He would touch
the bier and then there wouldn't be any corpse there!
He could do anything He wanted to do. If a sea was
tempestuous He went to sleep on the deck of the ship.
Somebody has said, "His sleeping there showed He was
human and then His calming the sea showed He was
divine." I think there is a flash of His divinity in the
fact that He could sleep. The disciples couldn't sleep.
How could He sleep? All the other people on the boat
were scared, but He was not scared. He stood there
and said, "Wind, cease blowing. Water, be still!" The
waves lay down on the bosom of the sea and went to

sleep like little babies sleeping in their mothers' arms.

He could do what He said He would do. He had power that nobody else ever had. He is the Son of God! He can "deliver the goods." He can give you eternal life. He is able and He is willing. He is dependable. He can do it. He will do it. He wants to do it! He said, "I am come that they might have life, and that they might have it more abundantly." When somebody wouldn't have it, He looked out and cried with a broken heart, "Ye will not come to Me, that ye might have life." Yes, He is able, and He is willing!

All right, how are you going to get this eternal life? You are going to get eternal life just as you get anything else. Everything you have you got one of three ways. Everything you have you got honestly, dishonestly, or had it given to you. You bought or stole or had given to you that textbook you have. You bought or stole or had given to you that coat you are wearing. You can't get anything any other way than by one of these three ways.

I said that one time and a man said, "I can." I said, "How?" He said, "I can create it." I said, "To create a thing you must have material out of which to create it; and that material you must get honestly, dishonestly, or have given to you." If you ever get eternal life you must buy it, you must steal it, or you must find somebody who can give it to you.

All right, let's buy it. What would you give for a lot up in heaven with a nice house right on the corner so you could see the angels pass to the right and to the left, where you could take in the whole view? What would some of our rich men give for that kind of an "estate" in heaven? There isn't a man on earth who would sell what hope he has of Heaven for all the world. The most blatant infidel who ever lived wouldn't sell his hope of heaven. A man may deny the existence of God, he may be an agnostic, he may be anything; but in the depths of his heart he has a faint hope that there may be a heaven and that somehow he may get there.

Men want to buy salvation. That is what is the matter with the world now. It is trying to find the means by which it can earn something that the Lord Jesus Christ wants to give away. The average man has an idea something like this: The angels are keeping the books up in Heaven. If he does a good deed it goes in one column. If he does a bad deed it goes in another column. When he dies the angels will add up the columns. If the good outweighs the bad he will go to heaven. If the bad outweighs the good, he will go to hell. That is the idea the average man has. But that isn't so. You don't go to heaven for doing good deeds and you don't go to hell just because you do something bad.

As a matter of fact, if you are a sinner you can't do good deeds. The Bible says that "all our righteousnesses are as filthy rags." The Bible says that though I give my body to be burned and do many other things and have not love, it profiteth me nothing. It may do somebody else some good. You might give this college a million dollars and be a sinner and die and go to hell. It wouldn't do you one bit of good as far as your salvation is concerned to give this college a million dollars. It might do somebody else some good. It profits *me* nothing to do good deeds if I am not righteous. The verse doesn't say it won't profit anybody else. It profits *me* nothing, even if I give all I have and then let my body be burned.

I am the son of a Confederate soldier. I grew up here in the South in the ragged end of reconstruction. I used to go to the political meetings. How pious those politicians talked—they wanted to be elected to office. The old Confederate soldiers would be there. Some politician would get up and make a speech. He would talk about Sherman's march to the sea. An old Confederate soldier would be sitting there. The worse the politician "cussed" the Yankees the harder he would peg the ground with his old peg leg. Another old fellow would beat the floor with his crutch and say, "Go it, Buddy! Go it! Go it!" Another old fellow would hit his leg with his one arm and say, "Hurrah for Dixie!" Then the speaker would get to telling about the great resurrection morning when the followers of Lee and Jackson would get up out of their graves. I could see in my mind those old Southern soldiers get up out of the graves, wrap the Confederate flag about them and march up to the gate! I thought until I was a big boy that all the Confederate soldiers were going to heaven and all the Yankees were going to hell!

Then I got to preaching in the North. I found some of those old men sitting in the front pew, the men who followed the flag in the Civil War, who marched down South and shot at my father and had my father shoot at them. They were wonderful saints of God!

But men don't go to heaven because they fight. A man doesn't get to heaven by dying for his country. That idea isn't Christian; it is pagan. The Japanese believe that. It isn't Christianity. All this is talk about a man's earning salvation. You can't earn it.

You can't pay for it after you get it! You can't buy it. Nobody could buy salvation except Jesus, and He paid for it with His blood. You can't buy it; and it is a cinch you can't steal it! Now, if you ever get it, you must get somebody to give it to you. And I can tell you *Who* can do it. I found *Him* when I was eleven years old and *He* gave me eternal life. There are mil‑lions on earth to whom Jesus has given eternal life.

I visited for a few minutes with a young lady student here last Sunday afternoon. I had heard her sing on the vesper program. I told her how I was praying for her. She said, "I have been saved since I came to Bob Jones College." Some of you since coming to Bob Jones College have received eternal life as God's gift. If you think you deserved it, or earned it, or can pay for it, you haven't got it.

Years ago I was speaking in a certain northern city. We had a large tabernacle and a great campaign. Thousands of people came. One night during the meeting hundreds and hundreds of high school young people were saved. If I remember correctly there were over a thousand of them that night who came forward on a definite invitation to accept the Lord Jesus Christ as their Saviour.

At the close of the service I started out of the side door of the tabernacle and met a woman. She was painted. It was back in those days before women pulled their eyebrows out; she had hers all penciled. Her hair was blondined. She said, "Mr. Jones, I just wanted to say that this was such a wonderful meeting tonight." I said, "Yes, it was a good meeting." You know, I can't stand women fixed up like that. They irritate me. Boys, whenever you see one fixed up like that you may know she is trying to make up on the outside for something she lacks on the inside. I started away and she said, "Just a minute, Mr. Jones. I just must say something that is on my mind and heart. Oh, it was the most marvelous meeting I ever saw." I said, "Yes, it was; good night." She said, "Just one more word, Mr. Jones. I just sat there and thought to myself as I watched all those young people come forward by the hundreds, 'After tonight that preacher can do anything he wants to do and he will certainly go to heaven when he dies.' You don't have to do anything else. It doesn't matter what you have done in the past or what you may do in the future, this one service is going to give you a home in heaven." I said, "You hush! You are trying to flatter me; but I am not going to flatter you. You have never been born again. You are on your way to hell! You are a miserable sinner without God. No person who was saved would ever have said what you have just said to me."

If you think you can buy it, you don't have it. "In my hand no price I bring," is the testimony of every saved person. "All my righteousness is as filthy rags," is the language of a man who knows God. You can't earn it. You can't pay for it. Nobody has it for sale. If you could pay for it you couldn't buy it. God is the only One who has it, and He has never sold it. "The *wages* of sin is death." The devil pays wages. You can buy death. "The soul that sinneth, it shall die," but *"The gift of God is eternal life."*

The Bible tells us there was one time a tricky sort of fortune-telling man who saw some men performing miracles. He walked up and said in so many words, "Say, will you cut me in on that? I would get rich if I could do all those stunts you are doing. I will buy it. What will you charge to teach me those tricks?" The servant of God turned around and said, "Your money perish with you! Do you think the gift of God can be purchased with money!"

Listen, when you have been in heaven a thousand years, you will walk up and down the golden streets of the City singing in your heart, "In my hand no price I bring."

Why, if you could wink your eye and earn salvation, you could walk down a street of gold in heaven and say, "I have a right here. Get out of my way! Don't you bother me." If some one asked, "How did you get here?" you could say, "I bought a ticket. I paid for my citizenship."

But when *you* get to heaven and walk down the streets of gold and somebody asks, "Have you any right here?" you will answer, "Oh, yes!" "How did you get in?" "Jesus gave me a ticket. I was broke; I didn't have a cent. I wanted to get up here and I didn't know what to do. *But I found Jesus.* I told Him I couldn't go to heaven, and He just reached out His nail-pierced hand and gave me a ticket. He said, 'Come on, here is a ticket for you. Just go on up there and make yourself at home." *"The gift of God is eternal life."*

A gift puts you under some obligation. If I give you a ticket to a program, there is a personal obligation of appreciation on your part. If you buy a ticket and pay your way in, you don't owe anybody anything. You have paid for your ticket. You can say, "I have a ticket. This is my business!" Any man in this town can buy a ticket to a program here at the college and walk in and sit down by his right. But if I give some one a ticket—if I say, "Here, you may have this ticket; I bought it and I will give it to you"—that puts that person under some personal obligation.

All throughout eternity you will be under personal obligation to Jesus. Young people, you can't buy salvation. You can't pay for it after you get it. But if you don't already have it, you can have it. Somebody is giving it away around here. His name is Jesus and He wants to give you salvation.

Before I stop I will use an illustration I have used many times, including a number of times here at the college. Maybe those of you who have heard it have forgotten it.

Do you see this quarter? I want to give it to you. But I am a peculiar man. I just give away quarters one way. I put a quarter in a book, shut the book, and offer you the book. You don't want the book? Well, all right, you can't have my quarter, then. I have a right to put the quarter in any sort of package I wish. You, of course, have the privilege of rejecting the quarter.

God has something He wants to give you. It is eternal life. He wrapped it in the most wonderful package you ever heard of. He put it in Jesus. People looked at Jesus. He had no form or comeliness; there wasn't anything about Him to be desired. And they didn't realize what was wrapped up in that package. They put Jesus on a cross. They nailed Him there. They killed Him. Then He rose from the dead, and He has been scarred ever since that time. If you could see Jesus today, the glorified, risen Son of God, you would find scars on His brow and scars in His hands. If you

could look at His side you would find a wound there.
His feet are scarred. But, say, He has wrapped up in
Himself a marvelous gift. God gives you eternal life
when you take Him. Eternal life is wrapped up in
Christ.

"He that hath the Son hath life." There is just one
difference between a Christian and a sinner. A Christian has Christ and a sinner does not have Him. That
is the only difference. *All you need is Jesus.* It is all
in Jesus! If you will take Him, He will blot out all
your sins. If you take Him, He will give you a new
nature. If you take Him, He will go with you along
the journey of life. He will be with you when you are
tempted. He will put arms of power around you and
give you victory. *"By grace are ye saved through faith;
and that not of yourselves; it is the gift of God; not of
works, lest any man should boast."*

Prayer: "Our Father, we thank Thee for eternal life,
the gift of God, which we have because we have ac-
cepted Jesus as our personal Saviour. If there happens
to be one in this building who does not have this eternal life, help such an one today to look up in the face
of Jesus and say, 'In my hand no price I bring. I just
trust Thee. I trust Thee as my Saviour *now.*' Help
some one to trust Thee right now if there is one here
who hasn't already done it."

Keep your heads bowed just a moment. While our
heads are bowed I wonder how many of you here this
morning could say, "I know I am saved. I know God has
saved me. I *know* it." Put your hands up. (Many
hands were lifted.) Isn't that wonderful? Take them
down. Now, while our heads are bowed and just before
we go, I wonder if there is anybody here who can say.

"I never saw this as I see it this morning, and I don't know whether I am saved or not. But right now, right where I am and the best I know how, I will trust Him." Put your hand up if there is anybody who will trust Him. Yonder is one hand. God bless you! And here is another hand. That makes two. Is there anybody else in this building, anywhere, who will say, "I never saw it just this way before. Now I think I understand, and right here this morning the best I know how I will trust Him"? Put your hand up where you are. I have seen two hands go up. Is there any other one anywhere? Yonder is another one. God bless you! Is there another one while our heads are bowed? I want to play safe about this. I want to be sure about it. Is there another one, anywhere?

Prayer: "Our Father, we thank Thee for these who held up their hands and said they knew they were saved and for those who say they have never understood it as they do this morning but that here and now they will, the best they know how, trust Thee. Help this school to be faithful to its testimony and never get away from the truth that the Lord Jesus Christ bore our sins in His body on the cross and that we have salvation in His Name and in no other name. Help us to magnify that Name. If we are saved, help us to realize that we are under obligation to Jesus. Help us to be faithful witnesses for Him, especially during these Christmas holidays when the world so needs a witness. We ask it all in His wonderful name. Amen."